BASEBALL'S MOST INCREDIBLE STORIES

Engaging Tales from Today's Greatest Players • Inspiring Values of Perseverance, Teamwork, and Integrity

MIGUEL CALOJERO

INTRODUCTION

Hey there! Welcome to "Baseball's Most Incredible Stories for Kids." I'm thrilled you're here because, just like you, I love baseball. It's not just a game; it's a way of life. I spent my youth playing baseball, which taught me much about teamwork, perseverance, and integrity. Those lessons have stayed with me, and now I want to share some amazing stories with you.

What's the purpose of this book, you ask? Simple. I want to bring you tales from some of the greatest baseball players ever. These stories are packed with fun facts, laughs, and valuable life lessons. We'll dive into the lives of players like Ronald Acuna Jr., Mookie Betts, Mike Trout, and many more. You'll see how they overcame challenges and became the stars they are today.

But first, let me ask you a few questions. Have you ever wondered what it takes to hit a dinger like Bryce Harper? Or what goes through a pitcher's mind when they're on the mound facing the best hitters in the league? How about the secrets behind the fastest stolen bases or the craziest catches? Well, you're in the right place. This book will answer all those questions and more.

Get ready for some cool sneak peeks. We'll explore how Shohei Ohtani manages to be an ace pitcher and a home run king at the same time. You'll learn about Jackie Robinson's incredible journey as he broke barriers and became a hero to many. Ever heard of Sadaharu Oh? He's the home run legend from Japan, and his story is nothing short of amazing. And of course, we can't forget Babe Ruth, the Sultan of Swat, whose adventures are legendary.

But wait, there's more! This book isn't just about stories. Between each chapter, you'll find fun educational stuff. Want to know how to compute a batting average? We've got you covered. Curious about the history of the Negro Leagues or the importance of integration in baseball? It's all here. We'll even talk about safe pitch counts for youth league players and tips for staying safe on the field.

So, what's unique about this book? For starters, it's packed with humor and fun facts that will keep you entertained. You'll learn about the players' quirks, like how Aaron Judge got his nickname "All Rise" or why Jose Altuve always seems to have a smile on his face. These stories are not just inspiring; they're also downright hilarious.

As you read, I encourage you to think about how these lessons apply to your own life. Whether it's working hard to improve your game, being a good teammate, or never giving up, no matter how tough things get, there's something here for everyone. These players faced challenges and made mistakes, but they kept pushing forward. You can do the same.

Before we dive in, I want to leave you with a personal note. Baseball has given me so much joy and taught me countless lessons. I hope this book will do the same for you. Whether you're a player, a fan, or just someone who loves a good story, there's something here for you. So grab your glove, put on your cap, and get ready for an exciting journey through the world of baseball.

CHAPTER 1: THE MODERN LEGENDS

Ever hear about a guy who can hit a baseball so hard it looks like it might never come down? Or someone who can run like the wind and make diving catches look easy? Welcome to the world of modern baseball legends. This chapter is all about the players who are making history right now. We're talking about the guys you've seen on TV, the ones whose jerseys you might own, and those who inspire you every time you step onto the field. These players didn't just wake up one day and become stars. They worked hard, faced challenges, and never gave up. They're like superheroes but in baseball gear.

Here's a cool question for you: What do you think it takes to become one of the best baseball players in the world? Is it all about natural talent, or is there more to the story? Well, you're about to find out. In this chapter, we'll dive into the lives of these modern legends. We'll explore their early days, their struggles, and their triumphs. And trust me, some of these stories are so inspiring, you'll be itching to grab your glove and get to work.

Ronald Acuna Jr.: The Journey from Venezuela to MLB Stardom

Ronald Acuna Jr. is a name you probably know well. But did you know that his journey to MLB (Major League Baseball) stardom started in Venezuela? Ronald grew up in a small town where baseball is more than just a game; it's a way of life. His dad, Ronald Acuna Sr., was a former professional baseball player. Imagine having a dad who knows all the tricks and tips of the game. Ronald Jr. learned from the best right in his own backyard. They practiced together, and his dad taught him everything he knew. But life in

Venezuela wasn't easy. The country faced many challenges, and resources were limited. Finding good baseball equipment and fields to play on was tough. But Ronald's passion for the game never wavered. Even at a young age, he showed signs of greatness. He had quick reflexes, a strong arm, and a natural ability to hit the ball. People in his town started to take notice. They knew he was special.

Ronald's path to the MLB wasn't a straight shot. It was filled with twists and turns, and he had to overcome many obstacles. He signed with the Atlanta Braves when he was just 16 years old. Moving to a new country and adjusting to a different culture was no small feat. Ronald faced language barriers and had to learn English quickly. Imagine trying to communicate with your coaches and teammates when you don't speak the same language. It was tough, but Ronald worked hard and never gave up. He also faced injuries and setbacks during his minor league career. There were times when he wondered if he would ever make it to the big leagues. But his talent and determination shone through. He rose quickly through the minor leagues, impressing everyone with his skills and work ethic.

When Ronald finally made it to the MLB, he took the league by storm. He won the National League Rookie of the Year award in 2018. He became one of the youngest players to steal 30 bases while hitting 40 home runs in a single season. His aggressive playing style and charismatic presence on the field made him a fan favorite. People loved watching him play because he brought so much energy and excitement to the game. Ronald's standout moments are too many to count. From hitting game-winning home runs to making jaw-dropping catches, he always finds a way to shine. His speed, power, and athleticism set him apart from the rest. Ronald's impact on the Braves has been immense. He's not just a great player; he's also a great teammate. He builds strong relationships with his teammates and contributes to the team's success. His dedication to improving his skills every season is evident. He works tirelessly to get better and never settles for less. Ronald also shows great sportsmanship and fair play. He respects his opponents and plays the game the right way. Off the field, he's involved in community and charity work, giving back to those in need.

Ronald Acuna Jr.'s story is a testament to perseverance, teamwork, and integrity. He faced many challenges but never lost sight of his dreams. He worked hard, stayed focused, and achieved greatness. His journey inspires us all to keep pushing forward, no matter how tough things get. So, the next time you face a challenge on the field, think about Ronald's journey. Remember that with hard work and determination, you can achieve your dreams too.

Mookie Betts: From Bowling Alleys to Baseball Glory

Mookie Betts is a name that sparks excitement. But did you know that before he was hitting home runs, Mookie was rolling strikes on a bowling alley? Yep, you heard that right. Mookie's early years were filled with bowling balls and pins, thanks to his mom, Diana Benedict, who was a competitive bowler herself. Mookie picked up a bowling ball even before he touched a baseball. Imagine that! His early years were a mix of different sports, but bowling was a big part of his life. He participated in youth bowling tournaments and even rolled a perfect game at the World Series of Bowling in 2017. The skills he gained from bowling, like hand-eye coordination and focus, translated perfectly to baseball. When he finally decided to focus on baseball full-time, it was clear that he had a unique set of skills that set him apart from other players.

Mookie's high school career was nothing short of spectacular. He played for John Overton High School in Nashville, Tennessee, and quickly became a standout player. His performances on the field caught the eyes of many scouts. Despite his smaller size at 5 foot 9 inches, he had incredible speed and a strong arm. These qualities made him a versatile player who could excel in multiple positions. In 2011, the Boston Red Sox drafted him, which was a dream come true for Mookie. But the road to the MLB wasn't all smooth sailing. He faced initial struggles in the minor leagues, needing to adjust to the higher level of competition. There were times when he doubted himself, but he never gave up. He made adjustments to his swing, worked on his fielding, and focused on improving every aspect of his game. His breakthrough moments came when he started putting up impressive numbers, which led to his promotion to the MLB.

Once Mookie made it to the big leagues, he didn't just participate; he dominated. In 2018, he won the American League MVP, cementing his status as one of the best players in the game. His role in leading the Red Sox to a World Series Championship that same year was monumental. He made notable defensive plays and showed incredible versatility on the field, playing both outfield and infield positions when needed. His stats are mind-blowing. He set records, such as being one of the few players to hit 30 home runs and steal 30 bases in a season. His batting average, on-base percentage, and slugging percentage were off the charts. But what really sets Mookie apart is his ability to make the game look easy. He plays with a level of confidence and joy that is infectious.

Mookie's career is a perfect example of perseverance, teamwork, and integrity. He faced early criticism and doubts about his size and ability, but he used that as motivation to prove everyone wrong. His leadership qualities shine through in the way he interacts with his teammates. He's always the first to celebrate his teammates' successes and the first to pick them up when they're down. His dedication to fair play and sportsmanship is evident in every game he plays. Off the field, Mookie is just as impressive. He and his wife, Brianna, created the 50/50 Foundation to help inner-city children in athletics, education, and life. Their foundation has made significant contributions, including donations to UCLA's Mattel Children's Hospital. Mookie's community involvement and charitable efforts show that he's not just a great player but also a great person.

So, what can we learn from Mookie Betts? His story teaches us that it's okay to have other interests and that those interests can make us better at our main passion. Whether you're into bowling, soccer, or any other sport, those skills can help you improve in baseball. Mookie's journey also shows us the importance of perseverance. He faced challenges and doubts but never let them stop him. He worked hard, stayed focused, and achieved greatness. His story reminds us that with hard work and determination, we can overcome any obstacle. And most importantly, Mookie shows us the value of giving back. No matter how successful you become, there's always a way to help others and make a difference in your community.

So, as you read about these incredible players, remember that they all started somewhere. They faced challenges, worked hard, and never gave up on their dreams. Whether you're aiming to hit home runs like Mookie Betts or make game-saving catches, know that you can achieve great things with dedication and perseverance. Keep playing, keep learning, and most importantly, have fun. The world of baseball is full of opportunities, and you have the potential to become the next great player. Let's get out there and make some memories!

WANT TO LEARN HOW TO CALCULATE YOUR BATTING AVERAGE?

You participate in 2 weekend games. On Saturday, you hit a homerun, a triple and a single in 4 at bats. To be exact, you had 3 hits in 4 at bats. In baseball jargon, you went 3 for 4. To calculate your batting average, you divide your hits (3) by your at bats (4).

3 ÷ 4 = .75

You have a .750 batting average!

The 0 is added because this means you would statistically have 750 hits for every 1000 at bats.

On Sunday you hit a double and a triple. You had 2 hits in 4 at bats.

2 ÷ 4 = .50

On Sunday you had a .500 batting average.

For the weekend you had 5 hits in 8 at bats.

5 ÷ 8 = .625

Your batting average for the weekend is a whopping .625!

You will be a star with a .625 batting average!

CHAPTER 2: THE POWER OF PERSEVERANCE

Ever think about what makes someone great at baseball? Sure, talent helps, but there's something even more important: perseverance. Imagine a player who never stops trying, even when things get tough. Someone who works hard every single day, no matter what. That's what perseverance looks like, and it's what makes players like Mike Trout stand out. In this chapter, we'll dive into the story of Mike Trout, a small-town kid who became a superstar because he never gave up.

Mike Trout: From Small Town to Superstar

Mike Trout grew up in Millville, New Jersey, a place known more for its cranberry bogs than baseball stars. Mike's family loved baseball. His dad, Jeff, played minor league ball, so baseball was in Mike's blood. Imagine having a dad who can teach you all the ins and outs of the game right in your backyard. Mike's mom, Debbie, was his biggest cheerleader, always there to support him. And let's not forget his community. Millville was like a big family that rallied around its local hero. Everyone knew Mike had something special, and they all wanted to see him succeed.

Mike played in local leagues and was a star at Millville High School. He practiced every day, even when his friends were out doing other things. He had this old pitching machine in his backyard, and he'd spend hours hitting balls. Some nights, he'd even hit under the lights his dad put up. His dedication was like something out of a movie. Coaches and teammates could tell he was different. He had that extra spark that made everyone believe he was destined for greatness.

When the Los Angeles Angels drafted Mike in 2009, it was a dream come true. But the road to the big leagues was anything but easy. In the minor leagues, Mike faced all sorts of challenges. He had to adjust to tougher competition, and there were times when he struggled. Imagine being far from home, playing against older, more experienced players. It wasn't easy, but Mike kept pushing forward. He worked on his swing, improved his fielding, and kept his focus. His performances started to stand out. Coaches noticed his speed, power, and ability to read the game. It wasn't long before he got the call-up to the big leagues.

The moment Mike got called up to the MLB is something he'll never forget. It was July 8, 2011, and Mike was just 19 years old. The Angels needed a spark, and they believed Mike was the guy to provide it. He made an immediate impact, showing flashes of brilliance that had fans and analysts buzzing. By 2012, he had a full season under his belt and was named the American League Rookie of the Year. He led the league in runs scored and stolen bases, proving he was a force to be reckoned with. From that point on, Mike's career took off like a rocket.

Mike Trout's MLB career is packed with highlights. He's won the American League MVP award multiple times, showing everyone he's one of the best in the game. He's led the league in various statistical categories, from runs scored to on-base percentage. Every season, he finds a way to amaze fans with his incredible plays. Remember that time he robbed a home run by leaping over the center-field wall? Or when he hit a walk-off homer to win the game? Those moments define his career. Teammates, coaches, and analysts all have high praise for Mike. They talk about his work ethic, his love for the game, and his ability to come through in the clutch.

But what really sets Mike apart is his perseverance and determination. He's faced his share of slumps and injuries, but he never lets them keep him down. When he's not playing, he's training and finding ways to get better. His offseason routines are legendary. He works on everything from his swing to his speed. He even studies game footage to find ways to improve. And it's not just about baseball for Mike. He's active in his community, always looking for ways to give back. He's a positive role model, showing young players that hard work and determination can lead to great things.

Reflection Section: What Can You Learn from Mike Trout?

Take a moment to think about your own baseball journey. What challenges have you faced, and how did you overcome them? Mike Trout's story shows that success isn't just about talent. It's about hard work, perseverance, and never giving up. Write down one or two things you can do to improve your game. Maybe it's practicing a little longer, working on a specific skill, or simply believing in yourself more. Remember, every great player started somewhere, and with dedication, you can achieve your dreams too.

Mike Trout's story is a perfect example of what it means to persevere. From his humble beginnings in Millville to becoming one of the best players in the game, he's shown that hard work and determination can lead to incredible success. So the next time you're feeling down or facing a tough challenge, think about Mike. Remember that with perseverance, you can overcome anything. Keep pushing, keep playing, and never give up on your dreams.

Aaron Judge: Overcoming Injury to Become a Home Run King

Aaron Judge grew up in the small town of Linden, California. His parents, Patty and Wayne Judge, adopted him when he was just a day old. They were always there to support him. Imagine having two parents who cheer you on at every game, who help you with practice, and who believe in you no matter what. That's what Aaron had. He wasn't just good at baseball. He played football and basketball too. He was one of those kids who seemed to excel at everything. In high school, he was a standout in all sports, but baseball was where he truly shined. He hit home runs that seemed to defy gravity and had a cannon for an arm. Scouts started to take notice. They saw something special in him.

After high school, Aaron chose to play college baseball at Fresno State. It was a big decision, but he felt it was the right one. College baseball was a different level of competition. It wasn't easy. There were times when he struggled. But Aaron didn't let that stop him.

He worked hard, stayed focused, and kept improving. His performances in college were impressive. He hit for power, played great defense, and showed leadership on and off the field. All this hard work paid off when the New York Yankees drafted him in 2013. But getting drafted was just the beginning. The minor leagues were tough. Aaron had to adjust to a higher level of play. There were slumps and setbacks. He faced pitchers who were older and more experienced. But Aaron kept pushing forward. He learned from every game, every at-bat, and every mistake.

Aaron's rise to MLB stardom wasn't without its bumps. His rookie season in 2017 was a roller coaster. He started strong but then hit a rough patch. He injured his shoulder, which affected his swing. Imagine trying to play through pain, knowing every swing might hurt. But Aaron didn't give up. He worked with trainers and coaches to get back to his best. And boy, did he come back strong. He broke the rookie home run record with 52 dingers, earning the nickname "All Rise" as fans stood up every time he came to bat. But the injuries didn't stop there. Over the next few seasons, Aaron faced more setbacks. He dealt with oblique strains, calf injuries, and even a fractured rib. Each time, he had to rehab and work his way back. It wasn't easy, but Aaron's determination never wavered.

Despite these challenges, Aaron's impact on the game has been huge. His rehab stories are the stuff of legend. He worked on his strength and flexibility by spending countless hours in the gym. He did everything he could to come back stronger each time. His leadership on the Yankees is undeniable. Teammates look up to him, not just for his talent, but for his attitude and work ethic. He's always the first to congratulate a teammate and the first to pick them up when they're down. His sportsmanship is top-notch, always showing respect to opponents and umpires. And let's not forget his community involvement. Aaron founded the ALL RISE Foundation to inspire young people to reach their full potential. He's involved in countless charitable activities, always giving back to the community.

Aaron Judge's story is a testament to perseverance and determination. He faced injuries that could have ended his career, but he never gave up. He worked hard, stayed focused, and kept pushing forward. His story shows us that no matter how tough things get, you can overcome them with hard work and a positive attitude. Whether you're dealing with a tough game, a tough season, or something tough in life, remember Aaron's story. Keep pushing, keep working, and never give up on your dreams.

In the next chapter, we'll explore the stories of players from around the world who have made it big in baseball. From Japan to Venezuela, these players show that talent and hard work know no borders. Get ready to be inspired by their incredible journeys and achievements. Stay tuned!

PERSEVERANCE

Continuing to strive to achieve your goals despite obstacles, failures, and difficulties.

CHAPTER 3: THE GLOBAL GAME

Ever wondered if baseball is popular in places other than the US? Surprise! Baseball is huge all over the world. Imagine playing baseball in a place where the traditions are different, the food smells amazing, and the fans are just as crazy about the game as you are. In this chapter, we'll explore the global side of baseball. We'll start with an amazing player from Japan who has taken the baseball world by storm: Shohei Ohtani. Get ready to meet a guy who can pitch like a pro and hit homers like a champ. Yes, you read that right. He does both!

Shohei Ohtani: The Two-Way Sensation from Japan

Let's start with Shohei's early life. Shohei Ohtani was born in Oshu, Japan. This isn't a big city like Tokyo or Osaka. It's a smaller town where everyone knows each other. In Oshu, baseball is a big deal. Shohei grew up in a family that loved sports. His dad played baseball, and his mom was a badminton player. Imagine having parents who can teach you how to hit a fastball and smash a birdie. Shohei started playing baseball in local leagues when he was just a kid. He showed talent right from the start. He could hit the ball far and throw it super fast. People in his town started to notice. They knew he had something special.

Shohei's training was intense. He practiced every day, rain or shine. His dad would help him with his pitching, and they would spend hours on the field. Shohei didn't just want to be good; he wanted to be the best. He worked on his hitting and pitching equally. Imagine trying to be the best hitter and pitcher at the same time. Most people would find that too hard, but not Shohei. He had a strict training regimen. He would wake up early, practice pitching, then hitting, and even work on his fielding. His dedication was unbelievable. He wanted to perfect every part of his game.

Shohei's career in Japan was nothing short of spectacular. He played for the Hokkaido Nippon-Ham Fighters in the Nippon Professional Baseball (NPB) league. From the moment he stepped on the field, he dominated. He could strike out batters with ease and hit home runs that left the crowd in awe. He quickly became one of the best players in the league. His stats were impressive. He had a low earned run average (ERA) and a high batting average. He even helped his team win the Japan Series in 2016. Shohei was a star in Japan, but he wanted more. He wanted to compete with the best in the world. So, he decided to pursue a career in Major League Baseball (MLB).

The decision to move to MLB wasn't easy. There was an intense bidding war among MLB teams to sign Shohei. Everyone wanted him. Imagine being so good that every team in the league wants you. But adjusting to the American style of play and culture was a challenge. Shohei had to learn a new language, get used to different food, and adapt to a new style of baseball. But he didn't let that stop him. He worked hard to adjust and stayed focused on his goal.

When Shohei joined the Los Angeles Angels, he made an immediate impact. In his first season, he won the American League Rookie of the Year award. He amazed everyone with his skills as both a pitcher and a hitter. He had historic performances, hitting home runs and striking out batters in the same game. People started comparing him to legendary players like Babe Ruth.

He broke records and set new ones. He became the only player to join the exclusive 50/50 club. He hit 50 homers and stole 50 bases in his debut year with the Los Angeles Dodgers in 2024. His ability to excel in both roles was something the baseball world had never seen before. He could pitch a shutout one day and hit a grand slam the next. It was like having two All-Star players in one.

Shohei's journey wasn't without its challenges. He faced injuries that could have ended his career. But each time, he came back stronger. His perseverance was incredible. He worked hard in rehab, stayed positive, and never gave up. He built strong relationships with his teammates and coaches. They respected him not just for his talent but for his dedication and hard work. Shohei showed great sportsmanship on the field. He respected his opponents and played fair. Off the field, he was involved in charity and community initiatives. He gave back to his community in Japan and the U.S., showing that he cared about more than just baseball.

Shohei Ohtani's story is a perfect example of perseverance, teamwork, and integrity. He faced many challenges but never lost sight of his dreams. He worked hard, stayed focused, and achieved greatness. His story teaches us that with hard work and determination, we can achieve our dreams too. So, the next time you face a challenge on the field, think about Shohei. Remember that with perseverance, you can overcome anything. Keep pushing, keep playing, and never give up on your dreams.

Jose Altuve: From Venezuelan Fields to World Series Champion

Imagine growing up in a place where baseball fields are just patches of dirt and old tires. That's what it was like for Jose Altuve in Maracay, Venezuela. Born in a city known for producing baseball stars, Jose faced his own set of challenges. He was always smaller than other kids. People doubted his potential because of his size. But Jose had a big heart and a love for the game. He played in local leagues on makeshift fields, often practicing with sticks and battered balls. His dad, Carlos, loved baseball and taught Jose everything he knew. They spent countless hours practicing, determined to make the dream come true.

Jose's small stature made him an easy target for skepticism. Coaches and scouts often overlooked him. They thought he was too short at 5’ 6” to play professional baseball. But Jose never let that stop him. He practiced harder than anyone else. He had a relentless drive. He showed up early, stayed late, and worked on every part of his game. His determination was unmatched. He would hit hundreds of balls, run drills over and over, and never complain. His dedication started to pay off. People began to notice that Jose wasn't just a small kid with big dreams. He was a talented player who could hit, run, and field with the best of them.

Imagine growing up in a place where baseball fields are just patches of dirt and old tires. That's what it was like for Jose Altuve in Maracay, Venezuela. Born in a city known for producing baseball stars, Jose faced his own set of challenges. He was always smaller than other kids. People doubted his potential because of his size. But Jose had a big heart and a love for the game. He played in local leagues on makeshift fields, often practicing with sticks and battered balls. His dad, Carlos, loved baseball and taught Jose everything he knew. They spent countless hours practicing, determined to make the dream come true.

Jose's small stature made him an easy target for skepticism. Coaches and scouts often overlooked him. They thought he was too short at 5' 6" to play professional baseball. But Jose never let that stop him. He practiced harder than anyone else. He had a relentless drive. He showed up early, stayed late, and worked on every part of his game. His determination was unmatched. He would hit hundreds of balls, run drills over and over, and never complain. His dedication started to pay off. People began to notice that Jose wasn't just a small kid with big dreams. He was a talented player who could hit, run, and field with the best of them.

Jose's accomplishments in MLB are nothing short of amazing. He has been a multiple-time All-Star and has won several Silver Slugger Awards. In 2017, he reached the pinnacle of his career by winning the American League MVP. He led the league in hits and batting average. His performance was crucial in helping the Astros win the World Series that year. Fans will never forget his walk-off home run against the Yankees in the 2019 American League Championship Series. It sent the Astros to the World Series and cemented his place as one of the game's greats.

But what sets Jose apart isn't just his stats. It's his embodiment of perseverance, teamwork, and integrity. He has faced slumps and injuries like any other player. But each time, he came back stronger. He never let setbacks define him. His leadership qualities shine through in the way he interacts with his teammates. He's always the first to offer encouragement and advice. His impact on team dynamics is immense. He's a leader both on and off the field.

Jose's sportsmanship and dedication to fair play are also

noteworthy. He respects his opponents and plays the game the right way. Off the field, he's involved in numerous community initiatives. He gives back to his community in Venezuela and Houston. He serves as a positive role model for young athletes. His story of overcoming obstacles and achieving greatness is an inspiration to many.

Jose Altuve's story is a perfect blend of hard work, determination, and success. From playing on makeshift fields in Venezuela to becoming a World Series champion, his journey is truly remarkable. His story shows us that no matter how big or small we are, we can achieve great things with dedication and perseverance. So, the next time you're facing a challenge, think about Jose. Remember that with hard work and determination, you can overcome any obstacle. Keep pushing, keep playing, and never give up on your dreams.

Ready to meet more incredible players from around the world? Stay tuned for the next chapter, where we'll explore the stories of other international stars who have made their mark in baseball.

ASMI (American Sports Medicine Institute) Guidelines Regarding Pitch Count for Youth Pitchers

The physicians and researchers at ASMI have developed some guidelines that parents should use to evaluate whether they are causing issues and/or injuries to youth pitchers.

Daily
7 & 8 year olds should limit pitches to 50 per day
9 & 10 year olds should limit pitches to 50 per game and 75 per day
11 & 12 year olds should limit pitches to 75 per game and 85 per day

Weekly
7 & 8 year olds: Not Applicable
9 & 10 year olds should limit pitches to 75 per week
11 & 12 year olds should limit pitches 100 per week

CHAPTER 4: RISING STARS AND ROOKIES

Ever wonder what it feels like to be a teenager and already be one of the best baseball players in the world? Imagine barely being old enough to drive, but you're already hitting home runs in the big leagues. Sounds unreal, right? Well, meet Juan Soto, the teen phenom with a mature approach to the game. His story is all about hard work, a lot of swings, and a love for baseball that started in the streets of Santo Domingo.

Juan Soto: The Teen Phenom with a Mature Approach

Juan Soto grew up in Santo Domingo, the capital of the Dominican Republic. It's a place where baseball isn't just a game; it's a way of life. Picture bustling streets, kids playing baseball with sticks and bottle caps, and the sound of cheers from local games. That's where Juan's love for the game began. His family played a huge role in fostering his passion. His dad, Juan Sr., was his first coach. They practiced in their backyard and even indoors when it rained. Juan Sr. threw bottle caps for Juan to hit, helping him develop quick reflexes and a sharp eye. From a young age, it was clear Juan had something special. He idolized players like Manny Ramirez and Robinson Canó, dreaming of one day becoming a star just like them.

Playing in local leagues, Juan quickly stood out. He had an exceptional ability to hit the ball, even when facing older and stronger players. Coaches and scouts started to notice his talent. They saw a kid who could not only hit for power but also had a mature approach to the game. He played with a focus and determination that was rare for someone his age. His dad's influence was evident in his disciplined approach and work ethic. Juan's family believed in him, and that belief drove him to work even harder.

At the age of 16, Juan signed with the Washington Nationals. Imagine that—while most kids were thinking about their next math test, Juan was signing a professional baseball contract. His journey through the minor leagues was rapid but not without challenges. He faced injuries that could have derailed his career. There were times when he had to sit out games and work through pain. But Juan's perseverance shone through. He stayed focused, rehabbed diligently, and never lost sight of his goal. His talent and hard work paid off as he quickly progressed through the minor league system. Coaches and teammates were impressed by his maturity and skill.

By the time Juan made his MLB debut at 19, he was ready. His impact was immediate. In his first season, he finished as the runner-up for the National League Rookie of the Year. He hit home runs, drove in runs, and played with a confidence that belied his age. His advanced plate discipline stood out. He had a knack for knowing which pitches to swing at and which to let go. This mature approach made him a tough out for pitchers. In high-pressure situations, Juan thrived. He delivered clutch hits and showed a calm demeanor that impressed everyone.

Juan's accomplishments are remarkable. He played a key role in the Nationals' 2019 World Series run. His performance was pivotal, hitting crucial home runs and driving in important runs. Fans and analysts were amazed by his poise under pressure. His ability to perform in big moments set him apart. He has a keen eye for pitches and a swing that generates tremendous power. These skills, combined with his mature approach, make him a special talent. It's no wonder he's been compared to some of the greatest hitters in baseball history.

But what makes Juan truly special are his values of perseverance, maturity, and leadership. Despite facing early career challenges, he stayed focused and worked hard. His leadership role on the Nationals is significant, even though he's one of the youngest players on the team. He leads by example, showing his teammates the importance of dedication and hard work. Juan also displays sportsmanship and respect for the game. He plays with integrity and treats his opponents with respect. Off the field, he's involved in community and charity efforts in the Dominican Republic. He donates to support young athletes and gives back to his community. His generosity and commitment to helping others are inspiring.

Reflection Section: What Can You Learn from Juan Soto?

Think about Juan's story and how it applies to your own baseball journey. What challenges have you faced, and how did you overcome them? Juan's story shows that success isn't just about talent. It's about hard work, perseverance, and staying focused. Write down one or two things you can do to improve your game. Maybe it's working on your swing, practicing your fielding, or simply believing in yourself more. Remember, every great player started somewhere, and with dedication, you can achieve your dreams too.

Juan Soto's story is a perfect example of what it means to persevere and stay focused on your goals. From his early days in Santo Domingo to becoming one of the best players in the world, he has shown that hard work and determination can lead to incredible success. So the next time you're feeling down or facing a tough challenge, think about Juan. Remember that with perseverance, you can overcome anything. Keep pushing, keep playing, and never give up on your dreams.

Julio Rodríguez: The Mariners' New Hope

Julio Rodríguez grew up in Loma de Cabrera, a small town in the Dominican Republic. Baseball was everywhere. Kids played in the streets, in parks, and anywhere they could find a bit of space. Julio was no different. He had a bat and a glove, and he loved the game. His natural talent stood out. Even as a kid, he could hit the ball farther than most of the older kids. His family was his biggest support system. They cheered him on at every game and practice. His community believed in him too. They saw his potential and knew he was destined for something big.

Playing in local leagues was where Julio started to shine. He faced older, more experienced players and held his own. Scouts began to notice his talent. They saw a kid who could hit, run, and field with the best of them. When the Seattle Mariners came calling, it was a dream come true. At a young age, Julio signed with the Mariners. This was the beginning of his professional career. It was a big step, but he was ready for the challenge. His hard work and dedication were about to pay off.

Julio's development in the Mariners' farm system was impressive. He quickly made a name for himself with standout performances. He hit for power and average, showing skills beyond his years. But it wasn't all smooth sailing. Early in his career, Julio faced injuries that could have set him back. He fractured his wrist during an outfield drill. This was a tough break, but Julio didn't let it stop him. He worked hard on his rehab and came back stronger. His resilience was remarkable. Coaches and teammates admired his determination.

In the minor leagues, Julio had many notable games. He hit home runs, made spectacular catches, and showed speed on the bases. These performances showcased his potential. Scouts and analysts began to talk about him as a future star. The moment he got called up to the MLB was unforgettable. Every kid dreams of that call, and Julio was no different. When the Mariners gave him the nod, he knew all his hard work had paid off. He was ready to show the world what he could do.

Julio's impact in the MLB was immediate. In his rookie season, he had key performances that caught everyone's attention. He hit home runs that left fans in awe and made plays in the field that showcased his athleticism. His power-hitting was a game-changer for the Mariners. He could change the outcome of a game with one swing. His fielding skills were also exceptional. He made diving catches and threw out runners with ease. Teammates, coaches, and baseball analysts praised his talent and work ethic. They saw a player who could become one of the best in the game.

What sets Julio apart is his embodiment of perseverance, teamwork, and integrity. He faced challenges head-on and never gave up. His resilience in overcoming injuries and setbacks early in his career is inspiring. He built strong relationships with his teammates and coaches. They respected him for his hard work and positive attitude. His acts of sportsmanship and fair play on the field were evident. He played the game with respect and integrity. Off the field, Julio was involved in his community. He inspired young athletes in the Dominican Republic, showing them that dreams can come true with hard work and dedication.

Julio Rodríguez's story is a testament to what can be achieved with talent, hard work, and perseverance. From his early days in Loma de Cabrera to becoming a rising star in the MLB, he has shown that anything is possible. His journey is just beginning, and the future looks bright. As you read about these incredible players, remember that they all started somewhere. They faced challenges, worked hard, and never gave up on their dreams. Whether you're aiming to hit home runs like Julio Rodríguez or make game-saving catches, know that you can achieve great things with dedication and perseverance. Keep playing, keep learning, and most importantly, have fun.

So, next time you’re on the field, think of Julio. Remember his journey and let it inspire you to keep pushing forward, no matter the obstacles. Stay tuned for more incredible stories as we dive into the tales of players who have faced adversity and come out on top. The world of baseball is full of amazing stories, and you're about to discover more of them.

TEAMWORK

A group effort to achieve an objective with common goals.

CHAPTER 5: THE INSPIRATIONAL COMEBACKS

Ever wonder what it takes to get back up after being knocked down? Imagine losing something so important to you, yet finding the strength to return stronger than ever. That's what this chapter is all about. Here, we dive into the stories of baseball players who faced big challenges and came out on top. Let's kick things off with Freddie Freeman, a player who showed the world what it means to come back stronger after personal loss.

Freddie Freeman: Returning Stronger After Personal Loss

Freddie Freeman's early career reads like a baseball dream come true. Drafted by the Atlanta Braves in 2007, he wasted no time climbing through the minor leagues. His talent was obvious. He could hit, field, and lead. By 2010, he made his MLB debut, and it didn't take long for everyone to notice his skills. Freddie quickly became a key player for the Braves. He was the guy you wanted at the plate in a clutch situation. His early career was filled with highlights. He racked up hits, home runs, and All-Star appearances. Fans loved him, and teammates respected him. He was living the dream, but life had other plans.

In 2012, Freddie faced something no one can truly prepare for: the passing of his mother, Rosemary. Losing a loved one is never easy. Imagine trying to play baseball at the highest level while dealing with such a profound loss. Freddie didn't just play; he excelled. He balanced his personal grief with his professional responsibilities. His family, teammates, and the Braves organization supported him every step of the way. There were moments of vulnerability, but also moments of incredible strength. Freddie showed that even when life throws its hardest punches, you can still get back up and keep fighting.

But Freddie's challenges didn't stop there. In 2015, he suffered a wrist injury that threatened his career. Imagine not being able to do something you love because of an injury. For a baseball player, a wrist injury is a big deal. It affects your ability to hit, catch, and throw. Freddie faced a long recovery process. There were days when progress felt slow and frustrating. But he didn't give up. He worked tirelessly on his rehab, determined to return to peak form. He battled through elbow inflammation and other nagging injuries. Each setback was met with perseverance and determination. Freddie's story is a testament to the power of never giving up, no matter how tough things get.

Freddie's triumphant return to baseball is nothing short of inspiring. He led the Braves to the playoffs multiple times, and in 2020, he won the National League MVP. His performance was stellar. He hit .341 with 13 home runs and an OPS of 1.102 during the 60-game regular season. His efforts didn't go unnoticed. Teammates, coaches, and analysts praised his resilience and skill. Freddie's memorable games and clutch performances post-recovery are legendary. He showed everyone that setbacks are just setups for greater comebacks.

Reflection Section: What Can You Learn from Freddie Freeman?

Think about Freddie's journey. What challenges have you faced, and how did you overcome them? Freddie's story shows that success isn't just about talent. It's about hard work, perseverance, and staying focused. Write down one or two things you can do to improve your game. Maybe it's working on your swing, practicing your fielding, or simply believing in yourself more. Remember, every great player started somewhere, and with dedication, you can achieve your dreams too.

Bryce Harper: Battling Through Injuries to Lead His Team

Bryce Harper's early career was nothing short of spectacular. Imagine being the first overall pick in the MLB draft. That's what happened to Bryce in 2010 when the Washington Nationals selected him. From the start, he showed he was a force to be reckoned with. In his rookie year, he won the National League Rookie of the Year award. Fans couldn't get enough of his powerful swings and fearless attitude. He quickly became one of the most exciting players in baseball. Harper's All-Star appearances and early career highlights solidified his status as a superstar. He was the guy everyone was talking about, whether for his clutch hits or his fiery spirit on the field.

But even superstars face bumps along the way. Bryce's career had its fair share of injuries. One of the first major setbacks was a knee injury. Imagine the frustration of being sidelined when all you want to do is play. The recovery process was long and grueling. He had to go through intense rehab, working every day to get back to his best. Then came shoulder and back issues. Each injury brought moments of doubt. There were times when Bryce wondered if he would ever get back to his peak form. Staying positive was tough, but Bryce showed incredible resilience. He pushed through the pain and kept his eyes on the prize. Stories of him working tirelessly to return to the field are both inspiring and humbling.

Bryce's journey to recovery wasn't a straight path. It was filled with ups and downs, but he never gave up. His rehab and training regimens were rigorous. Imagine waking up early every day to work on your strength and flexibility. He had a team of medical staff, family, and teammates supporting him. They believed in him and helped him stay motivated. Key milestones in his recovery journey were like small victories. Each one brought him closer to getting back on the field. Inspirational quotes from Bryce during this time showed his determination. He often said, "You have to believe in yourself even when no one else does." Those words kept him going.

Once Bryce returned to the field, he didn't just play; he led. His leadership and impact post-recovery were phenomenal. He played a crucial role in leading the Philadelphia Phillies to the playoffs. His performance was top-notch, and he won the National League MVP post-recovery. Imagine the feeling of coming back from injury and being named the best player in the league. Bryce's memorable games and clutch performances showed he was back and better than ever. He hit home runs, made game-saving plays, and inspired his teammates. Praise from teammates, coaches, and analysts poured in. They saw a player who had overcome so much and still managed to shine.

Bryce Harper's story is a testament to hard work and determination. He faced significant injuries but never let them define him.

His ability to come back stronger each time is a lesson for all of us. Whether you're dealing with a tough game or an injury, remember Bryce's story. Keep pushing, keep working hard, and never give up on your dreams.

In the next chapter, we'll explore the moments that define baseball. From historic games to unforgettable plays, these moments have shaped the sport we love. Get ready to relive some of the greatest moments in baseball history. Let's keep the excitement going!

BASEBALL CROSSWORD PUZZLE

Across

1. Former home of the Houston Astros
3. David Ortiz
6. Charlie Hustle
8. Japanese Home Run King
11. Homerun

Down

2. 3 Base Hit
4. Former Yankee Stadium
5. Nolan Ryan no-hitters
7. Babe Ruth Candy Bar
9. Home of the Braves
10. Los Angeles team

CHAPTER 6: THE HEART OF THE TEAM

Have you ever wondered what it takes to be the heartbeat of a team? Imagine being the player everyone looks up to. The one who lifts spirits when things go south and brings joy when things go well. That's what this chapter is all about. We're diving into the stories of players who are more than just talented—they're the glue that holds their teams together. Let's start with a powerhouse from Cuba, Yordan Alvarez. His story is full of challenges, triumphs, and a lot of home runs.

Yordan Alvarez: The Cuban Powerhouse and Team Player

Yordan Alvarez grew up in Las Tunas, Cuba. Picture a place where baseball is a way of life. Kids play in the streets, and everyone dreams of making it big. Yordan was no different. He loved baseball from a young age. His family was always there to support him. They believed in his talent and encouraged him to chase his dreams. But playing baseball in Cuba wasn't easy. The country faced many challenges, and resources were limited. Yordan had to make do with what he had. He played in local leagues and quickly stood out. His talent was undeniable. He could hit the ball far and had a powerful swing that left people in awe.

Yordan's journey to the MLB wasn't a straight path. He played in the Cuban National Series, the top baseball league in Cuba. But he wanted more. He dreamed of playing in the big leagues. This meant he had to make a tough decision. In 2016, he defected from Cuba. Imagine leaving everything you know behind to chase a dream. Yordan established residence in Haiti before signing with the Los

Angeles Dodgers. But his journey didn’t stop there. He was soon traded to the Houston Astros. This was a new beginning, but it came with its own set of challenges. Yordan had to adjust to a new culture, language, and style of play. But he was determined to succeed.

When Yordan debuted with the Astros, he made an immediate impact. It was like he was born to play in the big leagues. In his rookie season, he won the American League Rookie of the Year award. He hit home runs and drove in runs like it was second nature. His performances in regular and postseason games were nothing short of spectacular. Fans loved him, and opponents feared him. He had a knack for hitting clutch home runs and delivering when it mattered most. His power at the plate was unmatched. Yordan quickly became a key player for the Astros, contributing to their success in every possible way.

But Yordan is more than just a great player. He's a fantastic teammate and leader. He builds strong relationships with his teammates. They respect him not just for his talent but for his character. He mentors younger players, especially those from Latin America. He knows the challenges they face and helps them adjust to life in the big leagues. His work ethic is incredible. He’s always the first to arrive at practice and the last to leave. He works on every aspect of his game, always striving to get better. Yordan is also known for his unselfish play. He puts the team first, always looking to help his teammates succeed.

Yordan’s values of teamwork and leadership shine through in everything he does. He shows acts of sportsmanship and fair play on the field. He respects his opponents and plays the game the right way. His contributions to team success and morale are immense. He’s a key figure in the Astros' clubhouse, fostering a sense of unity and camaraderie. Off the field, Yordan is involved in community and charitable efforts. He gives back to his community and helps those in need. His story is a testament to the power of hard work, dedication, and selflessness.

Reflection Section: What Can You Learn from Yordan Alvarez?

Think about Yordan's story. What challenges have you faced, and how did you overcome them? Yordan's journey shows that success isn't just about talent. It's about hard work, perseverance, and staying focused. Write down one or two things you can do to improve your game. Maybe it's working on your swing, practicing your fielding, or simply believing in yourself more. Remember, every great player started somewhere, and with dedication, you can achieve your dreams too.

Yordan Alvarez's story is a perfect blend of talent, hard work, and leadership. From his early days in Cuba to becoming a key player for the Astros, he has shown that anything is possible with dedication and perseverance. His journey is inspiring and reminds us that with hard work and a positive attitude, we can achieve great things. So, the next time you're on the field, think of Yordan. Remember his story and let it inspire you to keep pushing forward, no matter the obstacles. Keep playing, keep learning, and most importantly, have fun.

Gerrit Cole: The Ace Leading by Example

Imagine growing up in Newport Beach, California, a place known for its sunny beaches and laid-back lifestyle. Now, picture a young Gerrit Cole, a kid with a dream bigger than the ocean itself. Gerrit loved baseball from the moment he could hold a ball. His dad, Mark, played a huge role in nurturing this love. They spent countless hours playing catch in the backyard. It wasn't long before Gerrit's talent started shining through. In high school, he was a standout pitcher. His fastball was so fast, you'd think it had wings. Scouts took notice, and Gerrit became the talk of the town.

High school achievements piled up. Gerrit led his team to many victories. His standout performances earned him a spot at UCLA, one of the top baseball schools in the country. At UCLA, Gerrit dominated. His pitching was on another level. He threw strikeouts like they were going out of style. By the time the Pittsburgh Pirates drafted him in 2011, everyone knew he was something special. But even with all his talent, Gerrit worked hard. He didn't take anything for granted. In the minor leagues, he honed his skills, learning the ins and outs of professional baseball. His journey to the big leagues was marked by dedication and grit.

When Gerrit finally made it to the MLB, he didn't just dip his toes in the water. He dove in headfirst. His breakout seasons with the Pittsburgh Pirates were nothing short of spectacular. He became the team's ace, the go-to guy in crucial games. His fastball, clocking in at over 100 mph, left batters shaking in their cleats. But Gerrit wasn't satisfied. He wanted to be the best. He was traded to the Houston Astros in 2018. Here, he reached new heights. His dominance on the mound was awe-inspiring. He struck out batters left and right, setting records along the way. In 2019, he set the franchise record for most strikeouts in a single season. It was clear Gerrit was at the top of his game.

In 2019, Gerrit signed a record-breaking contract with the New York Yankees. Nine years for $324 million. That's a lot of hot dogs at the ballpark! But the Yankees knew he was worth every penny. Gerrit didn't disappoint. His key performances solidified his status as one of the best pitchers in the league. He had games where he seemed untouchable, striking out batter after batter. His pinpoint accuracy and fierce determination made him a nightmare for hitters. Fans loved him, and teammates looked up to him. Gerrit's standout games are too many to count. Each one showcased his incredible talent and unyielding spirit.

What sets Gerrit apart isn't just his talent. It's his leadership and work ethic. He prepares meticulously for every game. He studies batters, plans his pitches, and leaves nothing to chance. His attention to detail is legendary. Younger pitchers gravitate towards him, eager to learn. Gerrit shares his knowledge freely, mentoring them and helping them improve. His calm demeanor in high-pressure situations is another hallmark of his leadership. When the game is on the line, Gerrit stays focused. This calmness spreads to his teammates, helping them perform better. Stories of his influence in the clubhouse are plenty. He's the guy who lifts spirits, offers advice, and leads by example.

Gerrit's values of teamwork and integrity are evident in every game he plays. He shows acts of sportsmanship and fair play, respecting his opponents and the game itself. His relationships with teammates and coaches are strong. They trust him and know he has their back. Gerrit plays a crucial role in fostering a positive team culture. He encourages everyone to give their best and supports them through tough times. Off the field, Gerrit is deeply involved in community and charitable efforts. Alongside his wife Amy, he has made significant donations to support various causes. Whether it's helping health workers or supporting local hospitals, Gerrit's commitment to giving back is commendable.

Gerrit Cole's story is a perfect example of what it means to be a leader. From his early days in Newport Beach to becoming a star in the MLB, he has shown that hard work, dedication, and integrity can lead to great success. His journey is inspiring and reminds us that with the right attitude, we can achieve amazing things. So, the next time you're on the field, think of Gerrit. Remember his story and let it inspire you to keep pushing forward, no matter the obstacles. Keep playing, keep learning, and most importantly, have fun.

INTEGRITY

A standard of moral and ethical values to live by.

CHAPTER 7: HISTORIC LEGENDS

Ever wonder what it would be like to be so good at baseball that people still talk about you almost a hundred years later? Picture hitting home runs so far that they seem to leave the stadium and maybe even the city! Welcome to the world of Babe Ruth, the Sultan of Swat. This guy wasn't just a baseball player; he was a legend. His story is one of transformation, talent, and a bit of mischief. Let's dive into the life of the man who changed baseball forever. Maybe have a Baby Ruth along the way. Yes, the candy bar is named after the star.

Babe Ruth: The Sultan of Swat

Babe Ruth, whose full name was George Herman Ruth Jr., had a rough start in life. He was born on February 6, 1895, in Baltimore, Maryland. Growing up, Babe was known more for getting into trouble than for playing baseball. His parents had their hands full with him. By the time he was seven, they decided to send him to St. Mary's Industrial School for Boys. This wasn't just any school. It was a reformatory and orphanage run by Catholic brothers. Imagine being a kid in a place where rules were strict, and fun was hard to come by.

At St. Mary's, Babe met Brother Matthias, a giant of a man who introduced him to baseball. Brother Matthias saw something special in Babe. He taught him how to hit, pitch, and field. Babe took to the game like a duck to water. He practiced every chance he got. It wasn't long before everyone at St. Mary's knew he was something special. Babe's talent was obvious. He could hit the ball farther than anyone else, and his pitching was nearly unhittable. It was like he was born to play baseball.

Babe's skills caught the attention of Jack Dunn, the owner of the Baltimore Orioles, a minor league team. Dunn signed Babe to his first professional contract when he was just 19. At first, Babe was a pitcher, and a good one at that. He joined the Boston Red Sox in 1914 and quickly made a name for himself. He helped the Red Sox win three World Series titles. But Babe wasn't just a pitcher. He could hit, and boy, could he hit! His power at the plate was unmatched. People started to notice that maybe his true calling wasn't just pitching.

In 1919, the Red Sox made a decision that would change the course of baseball history. They sold Babe to the New York Yankees. This move allowed Babe to focus more on hitting. It was a game-changer. Babe transitioned from being a pitcher to a full-time power-hitting outfielder. This decision didn't just change Babe's career; it changed the entire sport. Babe started smashing home run records left and right. In 1920, he hit a staggering 54 home runs. The next year, he broke his own record with 59 homers. By 1927, he set a new single-season record with 60 home runs, a record that stood for decades.

Babe's home runs weren't just hits; they were events. People flocked to see him play. He became a household name. His larger-than-life persona and incredible talent made him one of the first true sports celebrities. Babe's influence on baseball was immense. He revolutionized the game, making it more exciting and drawing in more fans. The 1920s became known as the "Golden Age of Baseball," largely because of Babe Ruth.

Babe wasn't just a baseball player; he was a cultural icon. He appeared in movies, endorsed products, and made countless public appearances. His name and face were everywhere. One of his most iconic moments came in the 1932 World Series. Facing the Chicago Cubs, Babe allegedly called his shot, pointing to the center-field stands before hitting a home run precisely to that spot. Whether he actually called the shot or not, the story added to his legend. Babe's influence extended beyond the baseball diamond. He inspired countless young players and brought joy to millions of fans.

But Babe's life wasn't all home runs and glory. He faced many challenges and personal struggles. Growing up in a tough environment, he had to overcome a lot to reach his dreams. Despite his rough start, Babe showed incredible perseverance. He dedicated himself to perfecting his craft and setting new standards in the game. Babe was also known for his acts of sportsmanship. He often mentored younger players, offering advice and support. Off the field, he contributed to charity and worked to grow the game of baseball. He visited hospitals, supported children's causes, and always made time for his fans.

Reflection Section: What Can You Learn from Babe Ruth?

Think about Babe's journey from a troubled youth to a baseball legend. What challenges have you faced, and how did you overcome them? Babe's story shows that success isn't just about talent. It's about hard work, perseverance, and staying focused. Write down one or two things you can do to improve your game. Maybe it's working on your swing, practicing your pitching, or simply believing in yourself more. Remember, every great player started somewhere, and with dedication, you can achieve your dreams too.

Jackie Robinson: Breaking Barriers and Making History

Imagine growing up in sunny Pasadena, California, where the palm trees are tall, and the opportunities seem endless. Jackie Robinson's early life was filled with challenges, but also with a lot of promise. Born in 1919, Jackie moved to Pasadena when he was just a baby. His family faced many struggles, but they stuck together. Jackie attended John Muir High School, where he quickly showed that he was a natural athlete. He wasn't just good at one sport; he excelled in many. In high school, he played football, basketball, and track, making a name for himself in each one.

After high school, Jackie attended UCLA, where he became the first athlete to letter in four sports: baseball, football, basketball, and track. Imagine being the best at everything you try. That was Jackie. He was a star on the football field, a powerhouse on the basketball court, and a speedster on the track. But it wasn't just about his talent. Jackie had a fierce determination and a never-give-up attitude. During World War II, Jackie served in the military. He faced racism and segregation, but he never backed down. His time in the Army only strengthened his resolve to fight for equality.

When Jackie left the military, he started playing professional baseball in the Negro Leagues with the Kansas City Monarchs. This was a big deal. The Negro Leagues were filled with talented players who weren't allowed to play in Major League Baseball (MLB) because of the color of their skin. Jackie quickly became one of the best players in the league. His speed, power, and skill caught the attention of Branch Rickey, the general manager of the Brooklyn Dodgers. Rickey had a bold plan to integrate baseball, and he saw Jackie as the perfect player to break the color barrier.

In 1945, Jackie signed a contract with the Dodgers' minor league team, the Montreal Royals. This was the first step in integrating MLB. The following year, Jackie played for the Royals and led them to a championship. His performance was outstanding, but he faced immense pressure and racism. Fans and players hurled insults at him, but Jackie kept his cool. He showed incredible strength and dignity, never letting the hostility get to him. On April 15, 1947, Jackie made his debut with the Brooklyn Dodgers. He became the first African American to play in MLB in the modern era. This was a historic moment. Jackie faced even more racism and hostility, but he continued to play with grace and skill.

Jackie's impact on the field was immediate. In his rookie year, he won the National League Rookie of the Year award. He led the Dodgers to multiple pennants and a World Series title in 1955. His speed on the bases and his ability to hit in clutch situations made him a fan favorite. But Jackie's influence extended beyond the baseball diamond. He became a symbol of the civil rights movement. His courage and determination inspired others to fight for equality. Jackie used his platform to speak out against racism and segregation, becoming a powerful advocate for social justice.

After retiring from baseball, Jackie didn't slow down. He continued to fight for civil rights and equality. He wrote columns, gave speeches, and worked with civil rights leaders like Martin Luther King Jr. Jackie's efforts helped pave the way for future generations of African American athletes and activists. He was a trailblazer, breaking down barriers and opening doors for others. Jackie's legacy as a civil rights leader is just as important as his legacy as a baseball player.

Jackie Robinson's story is one of courage, integrity, and perseverance. He faced incredible adversity and discrimination but never wavered in his commitment to breaking barriers. Jackie's resilience in the face of adversity is inspiring. He showed that with courage and determination, you can overcome any obstacle. Jackie's acts of sportsmanship and respect towards his teammates and opponents set a high standard for others to follow. He was a mentor and role model, teaching others the importance of fairness and equality. Jackie's legacy as a trailblazer and role model continues to inspire athletes and non-athletes alike.

Reflecting on Jackie's story, think about the challenges you face. How can you show courage and integrity in your own life? Jackie's story shows that you don't have to be a superstar to make a difference. You just have to stand up for what's right and never give up. Write down one way you can show courage and integrity in your own life, whether it's on the field, in school, or in your community. Remember, even small actions can make a big impact.

Jackie Robinson's story is a powerful reminder of the impact one person can make. From his early days in Pasadena to breaking the color barrier in baseball, Jackie showed us that with courage, integrity, and perseverance, we can change the world. His journey is a testament to the power of standing up for what's right and never giving up. So, as you face your own challenges, think of Jackie. Let his story inspire you to push forward and make a difference.

Jackie Robinson

JACKIE ROBINSON TRIVIA

Jackie Robinson signed his MLB contract with the

_______________ _______________

The General Manager who signed Jackie Robinson to a MLB contract was _______________ _______________

How many World Series championship teams did Jackie Robinson play on? _______________

What number did Jackie Robinson wear during his career? _______

Jackie Robinson began his professional career in the Negro Leagues with the __________ __________ __________

Jackie Robinson served his country in which branch of the military?

____

Which Brooklyn Dodgers teammate became great friends with Jackie Robinson?

_______________ _______________ _______________

Hint! He was referred to by 3 names. He also played shortstop for the Dodgers and was from Kentucky.

You can find these answers on an internet search with your parents.

CHAPTER 8: THE UNSEEN HEROES

Have you ever watched a game and thought, "Who's that guy who always seems to make the right play?" He's not always the star, but he's always there when the team needs him. These players are the glue that holds the team together. They don't always get the headlines, but their teammates know how important they are. One such hero is Corey Seager. He's the guy who quietly goes about his business, making key plays and leading by example. Let's dive into his story and see what makes him so special.

Corey Seager: The Quiet Consistency of a Champion

Corey Seager grew up in Kannapolis, North Carolina. It's a small town where everyone knows each other, and baseball is a big deal. Corey was the youngest of three brothers. His older brother, Kyle Seager, also played in the MLB. Imagine having a big brother who can teach you all the secrets of the game. Corey and Kyle spent countless hours playing baseball together. Their backyard was their own personal field of dreams. They practiced hitting, pitching, and fielding. It was clear from a young age that Corey had something special.

In high school, Corey played for Northwest Cabarrus High School. He wasn't just good; he was amazing. He was the number one baseball recruit in the state. Scouts from all over came to watch him play. They saw a player with incredible talent and a work ethic to match. Corey's performances on the field were nothing short of spectacular. He could hit for power, field with precision, and had a baseball IQ that was off the charts. His hard work paid off when the Los Angeles Dodgers drafted him in the first round of the 2012 MLB draft. It was the start of an incredible journey.

Corey's rise through the minor leagues was impressive. He had standout performances that made everyone take notice. But it wasn't all smooth sailing. Corey faced injuries that delayed his MLB debut. Imagine working so hard to reach your dream, only to have to wait because of injuries. It was tough, but Corey didn't let it stop him. He rehabbed diligently and stayed focused on his goal. When he finally made his debut with the Dodgers on September 3, 2015, he made an immediate impact. He hit the ground running, showing everyone why he was worth the wait.

Corey's early career was filled with key games that showcased his potential. He had a knack for coming through in clutch situations. His ability to perform under pressure was a big reason why teammates and coaches trusted him so much. Corey's consistency on the field was remarkable. He played every game with the same level of intensity and focus. His standout moments were many, but one of the most memorable was winning the National League Rookie of the Year in 2016. It was a testament to his hard work and dedication.

Corey's contributions to the Dodgers' success were immense. He played a key role in their World Series victories. In 2020, he was named the World Series MVP. His performances in postseason games were legendary. Whether it was hitting crucial home runs or making game-saving plays in the field, Corey always delivered. His stats are impressive. He's been named an MLB All-Star multiple times and has won several awards, including the Silver Slugger Award. But what really sets Corey apart is his dependability. Teammates know they can always count on him.

Corey's values of perseverance, teamwork, and humility are evident in everything he does. He's faced multiple injuries throughout his career but has always come back stronger. His role in building team chemistry is significant. He supports his teammates and leads by example. Corey's humble approach to the game is refreshing. He doesn't seek the spotlight; he just wants to play baseball and help his team win. Off the field, Corey is deeply involved in community and charitable efforts. He and his wife, Mady, have donated to various causes, including the renovation of youth baseball fields in Arlington. They want to give back and help the next generation of players.

Reflection Section: What Can You Learn from Corey Seager?
Corey Seager's story is an inspiring blend of talent, hard work, and humility. From his early days in Kannapolis to becoming a key player in the MLB, he has shown that with dedication and perseverance, you can achieve great things. His journey is a reminder that even the quiet heroes have a significant impact. So, the next time you're on the field, think of Corey. Let his story inspire you to keep pushing forward, no matter the obstacles. Keep playing, keep learning, and most importantly, have fun.

Corbin Carroll: The Emerging Star You Need to Know

Imagine growing up in Seattle, Washington, a city known for its rainy weather and passionate sports fans. That's where Corbin Carroll's story begins. Seattle is a place where kids play baseball in the rain and dream big. Corbin was one of those kids. From a young age, he showed a love for the game. His parents supported him all the way. They drove him to practices, cheered at his games, and believed in his potential. Corbin played in local leagues and quickly stood out. His speed and skill caught everyone's attention. By the time he reached high school, he was already making waves. At Lakeside School, he was a standout performer. He played with a level of skill and maturity that was rare for his age. Scouts started to take notice, and it was clear that Corbin had a bright future in baseball.

Getting drafted by the Arizona Diamondbacks was a dream come true for Corbin. Imagine being selected in the first round of the MLB draft. It's a moment that many young players dream of, but few achieve. For Corbin, it was the result of years of hard work and dedication. But getting drafted was just the beginning. The real challenge was just starting. The minor leagues are tough. The competition is fierce, and the road to the big leagues is full of ups and downs. Corbin faced several challenges as he adjusted to professional baseball. The speed of the game, the level of competition, and the pressure to perform were all new experiences. But Corbin didn't let these challenges hold him back. He worked hard every day, learning from his experiences and improving his game.

In the minor leagues, Corbin had several standout performances that showcased his potential. He hit for power, stole bases, and played exceptional defense. But it wasn't all smooth sailing. Corbin faced injuries that set him back. Injuries are tough for any athlete, but Corbin showed incredible resilience. He worked diligently on his rehab, staying positive and focused on his goals. Each setback was met with determination and a commitment to come back stronger. His positive attitude and work ethic were inspiring to his teammates and coaches. They saw a player who was not only talented but also dedicated to overcoming challenges.

One of the key moments in Corbin's career was his promotion to the MLB. It was a milestone that marked the beginning of his journey in the big leagues. Making it to the MLB is no small feat. It's the result of years of hard work and dedication. And Corbin was ready. In his rookie season, he had several key performances that highlighted his talent. He hit home runs, made spectacular plays in the field, and showed incredible speed on the bases. Fans and analysts alike took notice of his skills. He quickly became one of the most exciting young players to watch.

Corbin's impact in the MLB has been significant. His speed, fielding skills, and hitting ability set him apart as an emerging star. He has a unique combination of power and speed that makes him a threat both at the plate and on the bases. His ability to impact the game in multiple ways has earned him praise from teammates, coaches, and baseball analysts. They see a player who has the potential to be one of the greats. Corbin's memorable games and plays have already left a mark on the league. Whether it's a game-winning hit or a diving catch, he always finds a way to shine.
But what truly sets Corbin apart is his embodiment of perseverance, teamwork, and integrity. Throughout his career, he has shown incredible resilience in overcoming challenges. He has faced injuries and setbacks but has always come back stronger. His positive attitude and work ethic have been a source of inspiration to those around him. Corbin has built strong relationships with his teammates and coaches. They respect him not just for his talent but for his character. He plays the game with a level of sportsmanship and fair play that is admirable. Off the field, Corbin is involved in community efforts, inspiring young athletes and giving back to his community. He understands the importance of being a role model and uses his platform to make a positive impact.

Corbin Carroll's story is a testament to hard work, perseverance, and the importance of staying true to yourself. From his early days in Seattle to becoming an emerging star in the MLB, he has shown that with dedication and a positive attitude, you can achieve great things. His journey is inspiring and reminds us that even when faced with challenges, we can overcome them with hard work and determination.

So, next time you're on the field, think of Corbin. Remember his story and let it inspire you to keep pushing forward, no matter what obstacles come your way. Keep playing, keep learning, and most importantly, have fun.

HOME RUN LEADERS

Name the top three all time home run leaders in the MLB and the number of dingers they hit.

1 ______________________________

2 ______________________________

3 ______________________________

You can find these answers on an internet search with your parents.

CHAPTER 9: THE FUN AND LAUGHTER

Hey there! Ready for some laughs? Baseball isn't all about home runs and strikeouts. Sometimes, it's about having a good time with your teammates. Imagine this: you're in the clubhouse, and suddenly, someone jumps out of a locker dressed like a giant chicken. Believe it or not, pranks and jokes are a big part of baseball. They help players bond, ease tension, and keep the mood light during long seasons. So, let's dive into the world of MLB pranks and see how players keep things fun and hilarious.

The Pranks of MLB Clubhouses

In every baseball clubhouse, there's a tradition of rookie hazing and initiation pranks. It's like a rite of passage for new players. Imagine walking into the locker room to find your clothes replaced with a wacky costume. That's just the beginning. Veteran players love setting up elaborate practical jokes. These pranks aren't just for laughs; they help build camaraderie and trust among teammates. Take the story of Jeff Francoeur, for example. The El Paso Chihuahuas convinced him that his teammate, Jorge Reyes, was deaf. Jeff believed it for a whole month until he caught Jorge talking. It was a prank that had everyone in stitches and brought the team closer together.

Pranks play a big role in easing tension during those grueling 162-game seasons. Baseball can be stressful, and players need ways to let off steam. These jokes and pranks are perfect for that. They create an environment where everyone can relax and have fun. The laughter and camaraderie that come from pranks can strengthen team chemistry and morale. When everyone is laughing and having a good time, it's easier to face the challenges of the season together.

Some pranks in MLB history are legendary. What would you think if you walked into the clubhouse to find your locker filled with popcorn? That's what happened to a rookie on the Chicago Cubs. Veteran players filled his locker to the brim, and when he opened it, popcorn spilled everywhere. Another classic involves hiding equipment. One time, a player hid a teammate's glove, causing a mini-panic just before a game. Then there's the story of a player pretending to be injured. He limped around, groaning in pain, only to reveal it was all a joke. The entire team burst into laughter, and the mood lightened instantly.

The reactions and outcomes of these pranks are priceless. Players and coaches usually respond with laughter and camaraderie. Even the most serious coaches can't help but chuckle when they see a well-executed prank. For instance, when Joe Carter staged a fake giveaway of Derek Bell's new SUV, Bell was stunned. He thought his car was gone for good, but it was all in good fun. The prank ended with laughter and high-fives all around. Sometimes, pranks lead to memorable team moments that everyone remembers for years. Of course, not every prank goes as planned. There have been instances where things went a bit wrong and had to be resolved. But even those moments add to the team's story and bond.

Humor and fun are crucial in baseball. They help deal with the pressures of professional sports. Imagine the stress of playing in front of thousands of fans, knowing every move is being watched. Humor provides a much-needed break from that pressure. It helps players stay loose and perform better. During tough times, a good prank can lighten the mood and bring smiles to everyone's faces. It's all about balance. Players know how to have fun while still maintaining professionalism. They're serious when they need to be but know when it's time to joke around.

Some players are known for their sense of humor and ability to keep things light. These players are remembered not just for their skills but for the joy and laughter they brought to the game.

Reflection Section: What Makes a Great Team?

Think about your own baseball team. What makes your team special? Is it the way you all work together, or is it the fun you have off the field? Write down one or two things that bring your team closer. Maybe it's a funny tradition, a favorite joke, or a memorable prank. Sharing these moments can help you appreciate the importance of fun and laughter in building a strong team.

Baseball is more than just a game; it's about the friendships and memories you make along the way. So next time you're in the dugout or locker room, think about how you can bring a smile to your teammates' faces. Whether it's a harmless joke or a funny story, remember that laughter is a key part of the game. Keep the fun alive and enjoy every moment on and off the field!

The Funniest Moments in Baseball History

Baseball is full of moments that make you laugh out loud. Picture this: a player is running full speed towards first base. Suddenly, he trips and goes flying. It might be embarrassing for him, but for everyone watching, it’s pure comedy gold. Players tripping over bases or running into each other happens more often than you think. Sometimes, they even collide in the outfield, each thinking the other will catch the ball. It's like a scene from a slapstick comedy movie. These moments remind us that even the pros are human and can have clumsy days too.

Then there are the times when mascots get involved. Imagine a giant, fluffy creature running onto the field, causing a distraction. One famous mascot moment involves the San Diego Chicken.

Team celebrations and locker room antics also provide plenty of laughs. After a big win, the clubhouse turns into a fun zone. Players dance and sometimes play pranks on each other. One time, a player filled another's locker with shaving cream, and when he opened it, the foam exploded everywhere. The reaction was priceless. These celebrations are a chance for players to let loose and enjoy their victories. They work hard, and these moments of joy and laughter are well-deserved.

Baseball traditions and rituals have their own humorous side. Take the seventh-inning stretch, for example. Fans stand up, stretch, and sing “Take Me Out to the Ball Game.” But sometimes, things get a little wild. Fans might dress up in costumes, do funny dances, or start a wave that goes around the entire stadium. It’s a light-hearted break in the game that everyone looks forward to.

Players have quirky superstitions and rituals that can be pretty funny too. Some players eat the same meal before every game or wear their lucky socks without washing them for weeks. One player even wore his underwear inside out for an entire season because he believed it brought him good luck. These rituals might seem strange, but they add to the charm of the game.

Team photo days and media events are another source of laughs. Players often strike funny poses or make silly faces during team photos. They might photobomb their teammates or wear goofy accessories. During media events, players sometimes give funny answers to reporters' questions, keeping things light and entertaining. These moments show that even during serious events, there’s room for humor.

Mascots play a big role in keeping the game fun for fans. They perform crazy stunts, dance, and interact with both players and fans. One time, a mascot challenged a player to a dance-off and won! The player laughed it off, and the fans went wild. These interactions create memorable experiences for everyone at the ballpark.

Humor enhances the fan experience in many ways. It keeps the game enjoyable for fans of all ages. Whether you're a kid attending your first game or a longtime fan, funny moments make the experience special. Fans often get involved in the humor too. They might bring funny signs, wear costumes, or start chants that get everyone laughing. One time, a fan caught a foul ball in his soft drink cup. The crowd went nuts, and the clip went viral on social media.

Speaking of social media, it plays a huge role in sharing and popularizing funny baseball moments. Clips of players doing silly dances, mascots goofing off, or fans pulling off funny stunts quickly spread online. These clips get millions of views, bringing joy to people who might not even be watching the game. Social media helps keep the fun and laughter going long after the game is over. Some players are fan favorites because of their sense of humor and playful nature. Take Jonathan Papelbon, known for his legendary dances and funny antics. Or Yogi Berra, famous for his hilarious and often nonsensical quotes. These players bring more than just skill to the game; they bring joy and laughter. Fans love them not just for their talent but for the smiles they bring.

The funniest moments in baseball remind us that the game is not just about competition; it's also about having a good time. These moments make the sport more enjoyable for everyone involved. They create memories that last a lifetime and bring people together. So next time you watch a game, keep an eye out for the funny moments. They're an important part of what makes baseball so special.

Laughter and fun are a big part of baseball, both on and off the field. From players tripping over bases to hilarious interviews, these moments add joy to the game. As we move forward, let's keep the laughter going and remember to enjoy every moment, no matter how silly it may be.

NAME THE ALL TIME HITS LEADER IN THE MLB

Ty Cobb is second with 4,189 hits.
Hank Aaron comes in third with another celebrated record of 3,771 hits.

CHAPTER 10: THE TRAILBLAZERS

Ever wondered what it's like to be a superhero both on and off the field? Well, let me introduce you to a real-life hero who did just that. His name is Roberto Clemente. He wasn't just an incredible baseball player; he was also a humanitarian who helped countless people. Imagine being so amazing at baseball that you win Gold Glove Awards like they're candy. Now, picture yourself also helping people in need and making the world a better place. That's Roberto Clemente for you. Let's dive into his story and see what made him such a legend.

Roberto Clemente: The Humanitarian Hero

Roberto Clemente was born on August 18, 1934, in Carolina, Puerto Rico. Growing up, he didn't have much, but what he did have was a big heart and a love for baseball. Picture young Roberto, playing baseball with his friends in the streets, using sticks for bats and whatever they could find for balls. He played in local leagues and showed early signs of talent. People started to notice that he wasn't just good; he was great. He could hit, run, and field like a pro, even as a kid.

Roberto's talent caught the attention of the Brooklyn Dodgers, who signed him in 1954. But before he could play for them, the Pittsburgh Pirates drafted him. This was a turning point in his career. Imagine moving to a new country and facing new challenges. Roberto had to overcome racial and cultural barriers in the United States. People doubted him because he was from Puerto Rico and spoke Spanish. But Roberto didn't let that stop him. He worked hard and proved everyone wrong.

On the field, Roberto was a force to be reckoned with. He won multiple Gold Glove Awards for his exceptional defense. Imagine being so good at catching and throwing that you win 12 Gold Gloves in a row! Roberto was also a hitting machine. He achieved 3,000 career hits, a milestone that only the best of the best reach. His batting average was .317, and he was known for his consistent performance. Roberto's key contributions helped the Pittsburgh Pirates win the World Series in 1960 and 1971. People still talk about his clutch plays and game-changing hits. His most memorable moment might be his performance in the 1971 World Series, where he was named the Series MVP.

But Roberto wasn't just about baseball. He was deeply committed to helping others. He dedicated a lot of his time to helping underprivileged communities in Puerto Rico and Latin America. He believed in giving back and making a difference. Roberto organized relief efforts and charity work for those in need. He raised money, collected supplies, and even delivered them personally. In 1972, after a devastating earthquake in Nicaragua, Roberto organized a relief mission. Tragically, the plane he was on crashed, and Roberto lost his life. He died trying to help others, showing his true character.

Roberto Clemente's legacy lives on. The MLB established the Roberto Clemente Award to honor players who exemplify sportsmanship and community involvement. This award keeps his spirit alive and encourages players to follow in his footsteps. Roberto's family continues his work through the Clemente Foundation, helping communities and promoting education and sports. His impact goes beyond baseball. He inspired many to be better people.

Roberto's values of compassion, perseverance, and integrity were evident in everything he did. He faced discrimination and adversity with resilience. Imagine being judged not for your talent but for where you come from. Roberto stood tall and showed everyone the power of hard work and determination. He never gave up. His commitment to helping others and giving back to the community set a high standard. Roberto's acts of sportsmanship and respect on and off the field were unmatched. He treated everyone with kindness and respect, making him a role model for future generations of Latin American players.

Reflection Section: What Can You Learn from Roberto Clemente?

Roberto Clemente's story is a powerful blend of talent, hard work, and compassion. From his early days in Puerto Rico to becoming a legend in MLB, he showed that with dedication and a big heart, you can achieve great things. His journey is inspiring and reminds us that with the right attitude, we can overcome any obstacle. So, the next time you're on the field, think of Roberto. Let his story inspire you to keep pushing forward and to help others along the way.

Cal Ripken Jr.: The Iron Man of Baseball

Growing up in Aberdeen, Maryland, Cal Ripken Jr. had baseball in his blood. Imagine living in a house where baseball talk was as common as breakfast. His dad, Cal Ripken Sr., was a baseball coach and mentor. He taught Cal the ins and outs of the game. Picture young Cal, running drills and practicing with his dad and brother, Billy Ripken, in their backyard. Billy shared Cal's passion for baseball, and the two brothers pushed each other to be better. Early on, it was clear that Cal had something special. His dedication to becoming a professional player was evident. He practiced tirelessly, always striving to improve.

When Cal joined the Baltimore Orioles, he made an immediate impact. He debuted in 1981 and quickly became a key player. His early career was filled with highlights. He could hit, field, and lead. But it wasn't just his talent that stood out. It was his work ethic. Cal transitioned from shortstop to third base and back, showing his versatility. This move wasn't easy, but he handled it with grace. His willingness to adapt for the good of the team was impressive. Cal's determination and dedication were on full display when he broke Lou Gehrig's record for consecutive games played. Imagine playing 2,131 games in a row without missing a single one. That's what Cal did. His streak started on May 30, 1982, and continued until September 6, 1995. This record-breaking moment was a testament to his durability and consistency.

Cal's accomplishments on the field are legendary. He won the American League Rookie of the Year award in 1982, followed by the MVP award in 1983. These accolades cemented his status as one of the best in the game. Cal's key contributions helped the Orioles reach the playoffs multiple times. His memorable plays and standout performances are etched in baseball history. Picture him making a game-saving catch or hitting a clutch home run.

These moments define his career. Teammates, coaches, and baseball analysts praised Cal for his skill and dedication. They saw a player who gave his all every time he stepped onto the field.

But Cal's impact goes beyond his stats. His values of perseverance, work ethic, and integrity set him apart. He played through injuries, showing incredible resilience. Imagine having a nagging injury but still giving your best every game. That was Cal. His dedication to preparation and continuous improvement was unmatched. He studied the game, practiced hard, and always looked for ways to get better. Cal's acts of sportsmanship and fair play were evident on and off the field. He treated his opponents with respect and played the game the right way. Off the field, Cal was deeply involved in promoting youth baseball and education. He founded the Cal Ripken Sr. Foundation in honor of his dad. This foundation helps young people through sports and education programs. Cal's commitment to giving back to the community is inspiring. He wanted to make a difference, and he did.

Cal Ripken Jr.'s story is a powerful blend of talent, hard work, and integrity. From his early days in Aberdeen to becoming the Iron Man of Baseball, he showed that with dedication and perseverance, you can achieve great things. His journey reminds us that even when faced with challenges, we can overcome them with hard work and determination. So, the next time you're on the field, think of Cal. Let his story inspire you to keep pushing forward, no matter the obstacles. Keep playing, keep learning, and most importantly, have fun.

Cal Ripken Jr.'s story teaches us the value of perseverance and hard work. His journey from a small town in Maryland to becoming a baseball legend shows us that dedication pays off. As we move on, we'll explore more stories of players who have made a lasting impact on the game and beyond. Get ready to meet more incredible athletes who have faced challenges and come out stronger.

BASEBALL CROSSWORD PUZZLE

Across

3. Birthplace of Nolan Ryan
4. Birthplace of Yordan Alvarez
6. Birthplace of Pete Rose
8. Birthplace of Jose Altuve
10. Birthplace of Mookie Betts

Down

1. Birthplace of Hank Aaron
2. Birthplace of Corey Seager
5. Birthplace of Derek Jeter
7. Birthplace of Sadaharu Oh
9.Birthplace of Roberto Clemente

CHAPTER 11: THE INTERNATIONAL ICONS

Alright, let's talk about baseball legends who aren't just famous in their home countries but have also made waves around the world. Imagine being so good at baseball that kids in different countries want to be just like you. That's what these international icons have done. They've shown that baseball isn't just America's pastime; it's a global game. Let's start with a player whose name is synonymous with home runs in Japan: Sadaharu Oh. This guy isn't just a home run king; he's a baseball legend who has inspired countless players around the world.

Sadaharu Oh: Japan's Home Run King

Sadaharu Oh was born on May 20, 1940, in Sumida, Tokyo. Growing up in a bustling city with a rich culture, Oh had a unique background. His father was Chinese, and his mother was Japanese. Imagine trying to navigate two different cultures while growing up. Despite the challenges, Oh found solace in baseball. He started playing in high school, and it didn't take long for people to notice his exceptional talent. He had a powerful swing and a keen eye for the ball. His high school years were filled with home runs, impressive catches, and a growing reputation as one of the best young players in Japan.

Initially, Oh was a pitcher. He could throw fast and had good control. But as he continued to play, coaches noticed his incredible hitting ability. They decided to transition him from a pitcher to a first baseman. This was a game-changing decision. As a first baseman, Oh could focus more on his hitting, and boy, did he hit. His power at the plate was unmatched. In 1959, he signed with the Yomiuri Giants, one of the most famous teams in Japan. This was the start of his professional career, and it set the stage for a legendary journey in baseball.

Oh's career with the Yomiuri Giants was nothing short of extraordinary. He played for 22 seasons, from 1959 to 1980. During this time, he set the world record for career home runs with 868. Yes, you read that right—868 home runs! Imagine hitting that many dingers. Oh led the league in home runs for 15 seasons and in runs batted in (RBIs) 13 times. His achievements didn't stop there. He was named the Most Valuable Player (MVP) nine times. The Giants won the Japan Series 11 times during his career, including nine consecutive wins from 1965 to 1973. One of the most memorable aspects of Oh's career was his partnership with Shigeo Nagashima. Together, they formed the "ON Cannon," a duo that dominated Japanese baseball.

Oh's impact on Japanese baseball and his international influence are immense. He played a crucial role in popularizing baseball in Japan, inspiring future generations of players. His success transcended borders, earning him international recognition and accolades. He was inducted into the Japanese Baseball Hall of Fame in 1994. After retiring as a player, Oh transitioned to coaching. He managed the Tokyo Giants from 1984 to 1988 and later the Fukuoka Daiei Hawks (now Fukuoka SoftBank Hawks) starting in 1995. Under his leadership, the Hawks won the Japan Series in 1999 and 2003. Oh's influence extended beyond Japan. His achievements and coaching career inspired Japanese players aspiring to play in Major League Baseball (MLB).

Oh's success was rooted in his values of perseverance, discipline, and dedication. He had a rigorous training regimen that included unique techniques like his famous "flamingo" batting stance. This stance involved standing on one leg while awaiting the pitch, helping him generate more power in his swing. Oh faced challenges related to his mixed heritage. In a time when racial and cultural biases were prevalent, he had to prove his critics wrong. His perseverance paid off, and he became a symbol of excellence in baseball. Oh was known for his acts of sportsmanship and respect for the game. He played with integrity and treated his opponents with respect. As a mentor and ambassador for baseball, Oh has inspired countless young players to pursue their dreams.

Reflection Section: What Can You Learn from Sadaharu Oh?

Think about Oh's journey from a high school player to a baseball legend. What challenges have you faced, and how did you overcome them? Oh's story shows that success isn't just about talent. It's about hard work, perseverance, and staying focused. Write down one or two things you can do to improve your game. Maybe it's working on your swing, practicing your fielding, or simply believing in yourself more. Remember, every great player started somewhere, and with dedication, you can achieve your dreams too.

From his early days in Sumida, Tokyo, to becoming Japan's home run king, Sadaharu Oh's story is a testament to the power of perseverance and dedication. His journey is inspiring and reminds us that with hard work and a positive attitude, we can achieve great things. So, the next time you're on the field, think of Oh. Remember his story and let it inspire you to keep pushing forward, no matter the obstacles. Keep playing and keep learning. Always remember, baseball is about having fun!

Ichiro Suzuki: The Hit Machine from Japan

Imagine growing up in Toyoyama, a small town in Aichi Prefecture, Japan. This is where Ichiro Suzuki's story begins. Ichiro was born on October 22, 1973, and from a young age, he was all about baseball. His dad, Nobuyuki Suzuki, played a huge role in shaping Ichiro's early baseball years. They practiced every single day. And I mean every day. His dad would hit countless balls to him, making sure his son could field anything. Ichiro's dedication was unmatched. While other kids were playing video games or hanging out, Ichiro was out practicing his swing and fielding grounders.

By the time Ichiro got to high school, he was already a top prospect. He attended Aikodai Meiden High School, and boy, did he stand out. His skills were so advanced that scouts started to take notice. He had a unique batting style that combined speed and precision, making him a hitting machine. After high school, Ichiro signed with the Orix BlueWave in 1992. This was the beginning of his professional career. Playing in Nippon Professional Baseball (NPB), he quickly showed that he was something special. He hit for high averages and stole bases with ease. His early years with the BlueWave set the stage for what was to come.

Now, let's talk about Ichiro's move to Major League Baseball (MLB). In 2001, Ichiro signed with the Seattle Mariners. This was a big deal. Imagine moving to a new country where the culture, language, and style of play are all different. Ichiro faced many challenges adjusting to MLB, but he tackled them head-on. In his rookie season, he did something extraordinary. He won both the American League Rookie of the Year and MVP awards. That's right, he was the best new player and the best overall player in the same season. His speed, hitting ability, and defensive skills left everyone in awe. Fans loved him, and he quickly became a superstar.

Ichiro didn't stop there. In 2004, he broke the single-season hit record with 262 hits. Just think about that for a second. He hit safely in 262 different at-bats in one season. That's like getting a hit almost every time you step up to the plate. His key performances and moments during his time with the Mariners solidified his status as one of the greatest hitters in baseball history. He had a knack for making spectacular plays, whether it was a diving catch in the outfield or a clutch hit in a crucial moment. Ichiro's impact was felt not just in Seattle, but throughout baseball.

When we look at Ichiro's accomplishments, it's clear he's one of the best. He achieved over 3,000 hits in MLB, and when you combine that with his hits in NPB, he has over 4,000 hits. That's more than Pete Rose, who holds the MLB record. Ichiro also won multiple Gold Glove Awards for his exceptional defense. His ability to read the ball and make difficult catches look easy was second to none. Memorable games and plays define his career, and he's praised by teammates, coaches, and baseball analysts alike. They all talk about his work ethic, skill, and the way he played the game.

But Ichiro's greatness isn't just about his stats. It's about his values of perseverance, work ethic, and humility. Ichiro was relentless in his pursuit of perfection. He practiced tirelessly, always looking to improve. His humble approach and respect for the game were evident in everything he did. He never bragged about his achievements; he let his performance speak for itself. Ichiro showed sportsmanship and fair play both on and off the field. He respected his opponents and played the game the right way. Off the field, he was involved in community efforts, bridging cultural gaps between Japan and the U.S. He worked to inspire young players and promote the game he loved so much.

Ichiro's story is about more than just baseball. It's about dedication, hard work, and staying true to yourself. From his early days in Toyoyama to becoming a legend in MLB, Ichiro showed that with determination and a positive attitude, you can achieve great things.

So, the next time you're practicing your swing or fielding grounders, think of Ichiro. Remember his story and let it inspire you to keep pushing forward, no matter the challenges.

BASEBALL FACTS: AMERICAS FAVORITE PASTIME

- The Cincinnati Reds were the first professional baseball club. They were known as the Cincinnati Red Stockings.
- Baseball gloves were first used in 1875.
- Japan has played professional baseball for almost 100 years.
- Branch Rickey made many contributions to the game of baseball. One idea was using a full time preseason training facility for baseball.

CHAPTER 12: THE CLUTCH PERFORMERS

Ever wonder what it takes to be the hero in a baseball game? Imagine standing at the plate, the crowd roaring, and knowing that your swing could win the game. Sounds like a dream, right? For David Ortiz, or "Big Papi" as he's known, this was just another day at the ballpark. Let's dive into the story of a man who seemed to have ice in his veins and a bat that could change the course of history.

David Ortiz: The Legend of Big Papi's Clutch Hits

David Ortiz grew up in Santo Domingo, Dominican Republic. Picture a young David playing baseball in the streets with his friends, using whatever they could find for bases and bats. Baseball was more than a game; it was a way of life. His family supported his passion, even though resources were scarce. David played in local leagues and quickly stood out. Scouts saw his talent and potential. In 1992, the Seattle Mariners signed him. This was the first step in his journey to the MLB. But life wasn't all home runs and high fives.

David faced many challenges early in his career. He struggled to secure a starting position. Moving to a new country and adjusting to a different style of play was tough. In 1996, the Mariners traded him to the Minnesota Twins. He hoped for a fresh start, but it wasn't easy. David had to prove himself all over again. He faced injuries and inconsistent playing time. There were moments of doubt, but he never gave up. In 2002, the Twins released him. It seemed like his dream was slipping away. But then, the Boston Red Sox came calling. This was the turning point in his career.

Joining the Red Sox in 2003 changed everything. David quickly became a fan favorite. His powerful swing and clutch performances made him a hero in Boston. But it wasn't just his batting that stood out; it was his ability to deliver when it mattered most. The 2004 season was a game-changer. The Red Sox were down 3-0 in the ALCS against the Yankees. Things looked bleak. But David had other plans. In Game 4, he hit a walk-off home run to keep the Red Sox alive. The next night, he hit a walk-off single in Game 5. Suddenly, the Red Sox had hope. They went on to win the series and then the World Series, ending the "Curse of the Bambino." David's performance earned him the ALCS MVP award. He had become one of the greatest clutch hitters in MLB history.

David's ability to perform under pressure was legendary. Imagine being in a high-stakes game, the crowd on their feet, and knowing that your at-bat could change everything. David thrived in these moments. His approach to at-bats was meticulous. He studied pitchers, understood their tendencies, and knew exactly what to expect. His psychological resilience was unmatched. He never let the pressure get to him. David's confidence in the batter's box was evident. He believed in himself, and that made all the difference. Stories of his preparation and mental focus are inspiring. He would arrive early, watch tapes, and visualize success. Teammates, coaches, and opponents all praised his clutch ability.

But David's story is about more than just baseball. It's about perseverance, leadership, and sportsmanship. He overcame early career setbacks and proved his critics wrong. His leadership qualities were clear in the Red Sox clubhouse. He lifted his teammates, encouraged them, and led by example. David's sportsmanship was evident in his respect for the game and his opponents. Off the field, he was deeply involved in his community. He founded the David Ortiz Children’s Fund, helping kids in need. His charitable efforts made a significant impact and earned him the Roberto Clemente Award in 2011.

Reflection Section: What Can You Learn from David Ortiz?
Think about David's story. What challenges have you faced, and how did you overcome them? David's journey shows that success isn't just about talent. It's about hard work, perseverance, and staying focused. Write down one or two things you can do to improve your game. Maybe it's more batting practice. Or just practice running the bases. Remember, every great player started somewhere, and with dedication, you can achieve your dreams too.

David Ortiz's story is a testament to what can be achieved with talent, hard work, and perseverance. From his early days in Santo Domingo to becoming one of the greatest clutch hitters in MLB history, he has shown that anything is possible. His journey is inspiring and reminds us that even when faced with challenges, we can overcome them with hard work and determination. So, the next time you're at the plate, think of Big Papi. Let his story inspire you to keep pushing forward, no matter the obstacles. Keep playing, keep learning, and most importantly, love the game and all it offers.

Reggie Jackson: Mr. October's Heroics

Reggie Jackson grew up in Wyncote, Pennsylvania. Picture a young Reggie running around, playing sports with his friends, and dreaming big. He wasn't just a baseball player; he was an all-around athlete. In high school, he played football, basketball, and track, but baseball stole his heart. His talent was clear. Scouts noticed his powerful swing and speed on the bases. Reggie knew he had something special. After high school, he attended Arizona State University. There, he continued to shine, becoming one of the best players in college baseball.

Reggie’s college career led to him being drafted by the Kansas City Athletics in 1966. But life in the minor leagues wasn't a walk in the park. He faced many struggles, from tough competition to long bus rides. Reggie had to prove himself every day. He worked hard, focused on improving his game, and stayed determined. His early career highlights included some impressive home runs and standout performances, but it wasn’t all smooth sailing. There were slumps and setbacks. Yet, Reggie never lost sight of his goal. His perseverance paid off when he made it to the major leagues.

Reggie’s rise to "Mr. October" status began with the Oakland A's. In the 1973 World Series, he had key performances that showed his clutch ability. He hit crucial home runs and helped his team win the championship. This was just the start. When he was traded to the New York Yankees, his impact was immediate. Reggie became a force to be reckoned with. But it was the 1977 World Series that cemented his legacy. In Game 6, he hit three home runs in a single game. Imagine hitting three home runs in the biggest game of the year! Fans couldn't believe their eyes. This performance earned him the nickname "Mr. October" and established him as one of the greatest postseason players in history.

Reggie’s ability to thrive in high-stakes situations was incredible. His approach to at-bats in crucial moments was meticulous. He studied pitchers, understood their patterns, and knew exactly what to expect. Reggie’s mental toughness was unmatched. He never let the pressure get to him. His confidence in high-pressure situations was evident. He believed in his ability to deliver, and that made all the difference. Stories of his preparation and focus during postseason runs are legendary. He would arrive early, watch tapes, and visualize success. Teammates, coaches, and opponents all praised his clutch ability. They knew that when the game was on the line, Reggie would come through.

Reggie's career was also marked by his values of perseverance, confidence, and integrity. He overcame early career challenges and established himself as a star. His leadership qualities were evident in the way he inspired his teammates. He led by example, showing them the importance of hard work and dedication. Reggie's acts of sportsmanship and respect for the game were clear. He played with honor and treated his opponents with respect. Off the field, he was involved in community and charitable efforts. Reggie founded the Reggie Jackson Foundation, which focused on helping underprivileged kids. His contributions to the community made a significant impact and showed his commitment to making a difference.

Reggie Jackson's story is a testament to what can be achieved with talent, hard work, and perseverance. From his early days in Wyncote to becoming one of the most feared hitters in postseason history, he showed that anything is possible. His ability to perform under pressure and his commitment to excellence made him a legend. So, the next time you're in a high-pressure situation, think of Reggie. Let his story inspire you to keep pushing forward, no matter the obstacles.

In the next chapter, we'll explore the stories of players who faced incredible challenges and made unforgettable comebacks. Their journeys are filled with determination, grit, and moments that defined their careers. Get ready to be inspired by their resilience and never-give-up attitude.

44

COMMON SLANG AND LINGO

- Dinger: A home run. "He hit a dinger right out of the park!"
- K: A strikeout. "He struck out the side with three K's."
- RBI: Runs Batted In. "She had five RBIs in yesterday's game."
- Batting Average: A statistic that measures a player's hitting performance. "His batting average is .300 this season."
- Double Play: A defensive play that results in two outs. "They turned a slick double play to end the inning."
- Steal: Successfully advancing to the next base while the pitcher is delivering the ball to home plate. "He stole second base with ease."
- On Deck: The next batter up. "Who's on deck?"
- Bullpen: The area where pitchers warm up before entering the game. "The bullpen is warming up."
- Walk-Off: A hit that ends the game in favor of the home team. "He hit a walk-off homerun!"
- No-Hitter: A game in which a pitcher does not allow any hits. "He pitched a no-hitter last night."
- Slugger: A powerful hitter. "He's one of the biggest sluggers in the league."
- Cycle: When a player hits a single, double, triple, and home run in the same game. "She hit for the cycle yesterday."
- Caught Looking: When a batter is struck out without swinging. "He was caught looking at strike three."
- Hot Corner: Third base, known for hard-hit balls. "He's solid at the hot corner."
- Five-Tool Player: A player who excels at hitting for average, hitting for power, base running, throwing, and fielding. "He's a true five-tool player."

CHAPTER 13: THE LEADERS ON AND OFF THE FIELD

Ever think about what makes a great leader? Sure, hitting home runs and making crazy catches are cool. But what about the stuff that happens off the field? Imagine leading a team of legends and being the one everyone looks up to. That's what Derek Jeter did. He wasn't just a superstar; he was "The Captain." Let's dive into his story and see how he became one of the greatest leaders in baseball history.

Derek Jeter: The Captain of the Yankees

Derek Jeter grew up in Kalamazoo, Michigan. Yep, Kalamazoo—sounds like a fun place, right? His family was super supportive. His dad, Dr. Charles Jeter, was a counselor who helped people turn their lives around. His mom, Dorothy, worked as an accountant. Both of them made sure Derek and his sister, Sharlee, grew up with strong values. They believed in hard work and doing the right thing. From a young age, Derek knew he wanted to play baseball. He would tell everyone he was going to play for the New York Yankees. Talk about dreaming big!

In high school, Derek was a total standout. He played for Kalamazoo Central High School and quickly became a local hero. His skills on the field were insane. He hit for average, had speed, and his glove work was top-notch. Scouts started to notice. By the time he graduated, he had a bunch of awards and a lot of attention. The Yankees drafted him right after high school in 1992. Imagine getting a call from the Yankees at 18! Derek packed his bags and started his journey through the minor leagues.

The road to the MLB wasn't easy. Derek faced challenges that tested his determination. He struggled a bit in his first year in the minors. He made a lot of errors and had to adjust to the higher level of competition. But Derek didn't give up. He worked harder, practiced more, and focused on getting better. His determination paid off. By 1995, he made his MLB debut with the Yankees. It wasn't long before he became the team's starting shortstop. Derek's rookie season in 1996 was a game-changer. He won the American League Rookie of the Year award unanimously. That means everyone agreed he was the best new player. Not bad for a kid from Kalamazoo! But that was just the beginning. Derek's leadership on the field became clear. He played a crucial role in the Yankees' World Series victories in the late 1990s and early 2000s. They won five championships with him on the team.

One of Derek's most memorable moments came in 2001. It's known as "The Flip." Imagine Derek running from shortstop to make an impossible play, flipping the ball to the catcher to get the out. It was a game-saving play, and it showed his incredible instincts and leadership. Another iconic moment was his 3,000th hit. He didn't just get a single; he hit a home run. Talk about making history in style! Teammates, coaches, and even opponents praised Derek for his leadership qualities. They respected him not just for his skills but for his character.

Derek's impact wasn't limited to the field. Off the field, he made a huge difference too. In 1996, he and his dad started the Turn 2 Foundation. The foundation helps young people avoid drugs and alcohol while promoting healthy lifestyles. It's named after Derek's jersey number and the double play in baseball. Turn 2 has donated over $40 million to support programs and organizations that help kids. Derek's efforts have changed many lives, showing that he cares about more than just baseball.

Derek also launched The Players' Tribune. This platform allows athletes to share their stories in their own words. It's a way for them to connect with fans and share their experiences. Derek's idea helped athletes have a voice and tell their stories. His community involvement didn't stop there. He participated in countless charity events and always found ways to give back. Whether in New York or his hometown, Derek made sure to help out. His actions off the field inspired many young athletes to follow his lead.

Derek Jeter's story is all about integrity, humility, and perseverance. He always played the game the right way. He respected his opponents and never showed up the other team. Even when he was in a slump or dealing with injuries, he stayed positive and worked hard to bounce back. His humble approach made him a favorite among fans and an inspiration to many. Derek didn't just want to be the best player; he wanted to be the best person he could be. His perseverance through tough times showed his true character.

So, what can you learn from Derek Jeter? Think about how he handled challenges and led by example. Reflect on your own actions and how you can be a better teammate and leader. Whether on the field or in life, Derek's story shows that doing the right thing and working hard pays off. Keep pushing, stay humble, and always strive to be the best version of yourself.

Clayton Kershaw: Excellence and Integrity

Clayton Kershaw grew up in Dallas, Texas. Picture a young boy with a baseball glove almost bigger than him. That was Clayton. His family was super supportive, and their faith was a big part of their lives. His parents, Marianne and Christopher, made sure he grew up with strong values. They encouraged him to chase his dreams but always to stay humble. Clayton's love for baseball started early. He spent countless hours practicing in the backyard, perfecting his pitch. His hard work paid off when he joined the Highland Park High School baseball team.

In high school, Clayton was a standout. He threw heat, striking out batters left and right. Scouts started taking notice. By the time he graduated, he was one of the top prospects in the country. The Los Angeles Dodgers saw his potential and drafted him in the first round in 2006. Imagine being just out of high school and already on your way to the big leagues! But getting drafted was just the beginning. Clayton had to prove himself in the minor leagues. He faced tough competition and had to adjust to the higher level of play. There were times when he struggled, but he never gave up. His determination and hard work paid off, and by 2008, he was called up to the MLB.

Clayton's rise to ace status was nothing short of spectacular. He quickly established himself as one of the best pitchers in the league. He won his first Cy Young Award in 2011, and that was just the start. He went on to win two more, in 2013 and 2014. These awards are given to the best pitcher in each league, and Clayton earned them with his dominant performances. He had key performances in both regular season and postseason games. His no-hitters are legendary. Imagine pitching a game where the other team doesn't get a single hit! Clayton did that twice, once in 2014 and again in 2015. These moments not only define his career but also show his incredible skill and focus.

Teammates, coaches, and opponents praised Clayton for his leadership qualities. He wasn't just a great pitcher; he was a great teammate. He led by example, always working hard and staying positive. His dedication to the game and his team was clear. He was the first to arrive at practice and the last to leave. His work ethic inspired everyone around him. Even when things got tough, Clayton stayed focused and kept pushing forward. His leadership on the field was matched by his integrity and sportsmanship. He played the game the right way and always showed respect to his opponents.

Off the field, Clayton made a huge impact. He founded Kershaw's Challenge, a charitable organization focused on helping at-risk children and communities. Clayton and his wife, Ellen, traveled to Zambia, where they helped build schools and provide resources for children in need. They didn't just throw money at problems; they got involved and made a real difference. Clayton's work in Zambia is just one example of his commitment to helping others. He's also deeply involved in community efforts in Los Angeles and his hometown of Dallas. Whether it's building playgrounds or hosting baseball clinics, Clayton is always looking for ways to give back.

Clayton's values of integrity, work ethic, and humility shine through in everything he does. He prepares diligently for every game, always looking for ways to improve. He studies his opponents, practices his pitches, and stays in top physical shape. His commitment to excellence is unwavering. But it's not just about baseball for Clayton. He treats everyone with respect and always plays fair. He knows that being a great player means more than just stats. It means being a great person too. His humility is evident in how he interacts with fans, teammates, and even opponents. He's always willing to lend a hand, share his knowledge, and support others.

So, what can you learn from Clayton Kershaw? Think about his dedication and how he never gave up, even when things got tough. Reflect on your own actions and how you can be a better player and person. Clayton's story shows that integrity, hard work, and humility can lead to great things whether it's playing the great game or your everyday life. Keep pushing, stay humble, and always work to be your best in every aspect of your life.

WORLD SERIES

The New York Yankees have won 27 World Series since 1903. In second place for most World Series rings is the St. Louis Cardinals with 11. The Boston Red Sox and Oakland A's each have 9 World Series rings.

CHAPTER 14: THE RECORD BREAKERS

Ever wonder what it would be like to break a record that people thought would never be broken? Imagine being so good at something that you become the best ever. That's what Hank Aaron did in baseball. He didn't just hit home runs. He smashed records and faced down challenges that would make most people quit. Let's dive into the life of the amazing Hank Aaron, also known as "The Home Run King."

Hank Aaron: The Home Run King

Hank Aaron, born Henry Louis Aaron, came into the world on February 5, 1934, in Mobile, Alabama. Growing up in the racially segregated South, Hank faced many challenges. Mobile was a place where opportunities for black kids were limited. But Hank had something special: a deep love for baseball. His family supported him, even when times were tough. They didn't have much, but they made sure Hank could play the game he loved. Imagine playing baseball with sticks and makeshift balls. That's how Hank started. He played in local leagues, showing early signs of his exceptional talent.

As a teenager, Hank joined the Indianapolis Clowns of the Negro American League in 1952. This was a big deal. The Negro Leagues were where many black players showed their skills before integration in Major League Baseball (MLB). Hank's time with the Clowns was short but impactful. He played so well that the Boston Braves bought his contract. This move set the stage for Hank's legendary career. He started in the minor leagues, but it wasn't long before he was called up to the majors. In 1954, Hank made his MLB debut with the Milwaukee Braves. This was the beginning of a career that would change baseball forever.

Hank's pursuit of the home run record was nothing short of epic. Early in his career, he showed he had the power and skill to hit home runs. He steadily climbed the home run leaderboard, year after year. But it wasn't just about hitting homers. Hank faced intense media scrutiny and racial hostility. As he got closer to Babe Ruth's record of 714 home runs, the pressure mounted. Hank did not receive a lot of respect for his performance. Imagine trying to focus on playing baseball with all that going on. But Hank never let it get to him. He stayed focused and determined.

The key home runs came one after another, bringing Hank closer to the record. Then, on April 8, 1974, history was made. In a game against the Los Angeles Dodgers, Hank hit his 715th home run, breaking Babe Ruth's long-standing record. The crowd erupted in cheers. Two fans even ran onto the field to congratulate him. It was a moment that will forever be remembered in baseball history. Hank's strength and grace in that moment showed the world what a true champion looks like. He went on to hit 755 career home runs, a record that stood for over three decades.

Hank's impact on the game and his legacy as a record breaker is immense. He didn't just break records; he set new standards. His 755 career home runs were a testament to his skill and consistency. He made 25 All-Star appearances and won multiple MVP awards. Teammates and coaches praised him for his excellence and consistency. Analysts and fans admired his ability to perform at the highest level year after year. Hank's contributions to baseball are still felt today. His story inspires players and fans alike to strive for greatness.

But Hank's story is also about more than just baseball. It's about perseverance, dignity, and resilience. He faced racism and adversity with grace. Hank never let the hate and negativity stop him. He showed the world that you can achieve great things, no matter the obstacles. His unwavering commitment to excellence and continuous improvement is a lesson for us all. Hank also showed great sportsmanship and respect for the game. He played with honor and integrity, earning the respect of everyone who watched him play.

Hank was also deeply involved in his community and efforts to advance civil rights and equality. After retiring from baseball, he continued to advocate for social change. He worked to create opportunities for young black athletes and promote equality in sports. Hank received the Presidential Medal of Freedom in 2002 for his advocacy work. His legacy goes beyond baseball. It touches all who believe in justice and equality. Hank Aaron's life and career remind us of the power of perseverance and the importance of standing up for what is right.

Reflection Section: What Can You Learn from Hank Aaron?

Take a moment to think about the challenges Hank faced and how he overcame them. Reflect on your own life. What obstacles have you encountered, and how did you handle them? Write down one or two ways you can improve your game or your mindset. Remember, success isn't just about talent. It's about hard work, determination, and never giving up. Hank's story shows us that with perseverance, we can achieve great things, no matter the challenges we face.

Hank Aaron's journey from Mobile, Alabama, to becoming the Home Run King is a story of grit, resilience, and excellence. His achievements on the field and his contributions off the field have left a lasting impact on the world of baseball and beyond. So, the next time you face a challenge, think of Hank. Let his story inspire you to keep pushing forward, to never give up, and to always strive for greatness.

Hank Aaron

Nolan Ryan: The Strikeout Sensation

Nolan Ryan grew up in the small town of Alvin, Texas. Imagine fields of grass, lots of space to play, and a community that loved sports. Nolan discovered his love for baseball at a young age. His dad, Lynn, built a backstop in their backyard, and that's where Nolan started pitching. He'd throw for hours, working on his speed and control. By the time he got to Alvin High School, everyone knew he had a cannon for an arm. He pitched so well that scouts started to take notice. His high school games were like mini-events, with people coming just to see him pitch.

In 1965, the New York Mets drafted Nolan in the 12th round. It was a big moment, but it was also just the beginning. The minor leagues were tough. Imagine long bus rides, small paychecks, and lots of competition. Nolan struggled at first. His control wasn't great, and he walked a lot of batters. But he didn't let that stop him. He worked on his pitching, trying to get better every day. By 1966, he made his big-league debut. It wasn't smooth sailing at first. He had ups and downs, but the Mets saw his potential. They knew he had something special.

Nolan's career took off when he joined the California Angels in 1972. He quickly developed into a dominant pitcher. Imagine facing a guy who throws over 100 mph and has a wicked curveball. Batters were terrified. Nolan set the single-season strikeout record in 1973 with 383 strikeouts. Let that sink in—383! It's a record that still stands today. He had games where he struck out 19 or 20 batters. He became known as the Strikeout King. But it wasn't just about the strikeouts. Nolan was a workhorse. He pitched deep into games, often going nine innings and beyond. This earned him the nickname "the Ryan Express".

Throughout his career, Nolan faced many challenges. He dealt with injuries, like a sore arm and back issues. But he never gave up. He kept working, kept pitching, and kept striking out batters. His dedication paid off. In 1983, he achieved a milestone that still stands today—5,714 career strikeouts. No one has come close to breaking that record. Imagine striking out that many batters. It's like facing every kid in your school and striking them all out, and then some. Nolan's ability to strike out batters was unmatched.

Nolan's impact on the game goes beyond strikeouts. He pitched seven no-hitters, the most in MLB history. Imagine not allowing a single hit in a game, and then doing it six more times. Nolan did that. He also had multiple All-Star appearances and even won MVP awards. His performances were legendary. Fans would come to games just to see him pitch. Teammates and coaches praised him for his durability and dominance. Analysts called him one of the greatest pitchers of all time. Nolan's games were like must-see TV. You never knew what amazing feat he might achieve next.

Nolan's values of perseverance, work ethic, and integrity are what set him apart. He had a rigorous training regimen. He worked out, practiced, and studied the game. He wanted to be the best, and he put in the effort to get there. Nolan overcame injuries and setbacks. He didn't let them define him. Instead, he used them as motivation to get better. He showed great sportsmanship and respect for the game. He played the right way, always giving his best effort. Nolan also worked to mentor young pitchers. He shared his knowledge and experience, helping the next generation of players.

Nolan's community involvement is another testament to his character. He gave back to the sport and to those who supported him. He worked with kids, teaching them the fundamentals of pitching. Nolan wanted to see others succeed, just as he had. His legacy is not just about the records he set, but also the lives he touched. He showed that with hard work and determination, you can achieve great things. Nolan's story is an inspiration to all who dream of playing baseball. It shows that no matter where you start, with dedication and effort, you can reach the top.

Nolan Ryan's journey from Alvin, Texas, to becoming the Strikeout Sensation is a story of hard work, resilience, and excellence. His achievements on the field and his contributions off the field have left a lasting impact on the world of baseball. His story reminds us of the importance of perseverance, dedication, and giving back. As we move forward, think about the lessons from Nolan's career. Let them inspire you to work hard, stay focused, and always strive for greatness.

Next up, we'll dive into the unforgettable moments in baseball history that have left fans in awe. Get ready to relive some of the most exciting and heart-pounding events in the game!

BASEBALL PARKS

Boston's Fenway Park and Chicago's Wrigley Field have hosted professional baseball for over 100 years. Rickwood Field in Birmingham, Alabama, is the oldest baseball field in the USA.

CHAPTER 15: THE INSPIRATIONAL UNDERDOGS

Ever felt like the smallest kid on the team? Like no one notices you because you're not the biggest or the fastest? Well, meet David Eckstein. This guy was the underdog of underdogs. Growing up in Sanford, Florida, David was always one of the smallest players on the field. Imagine standing next to teammates who look like giants. But David had something special: an unbreakable spirit and a love for the game that couldn't be measured by height.

David Eckstein: The Undersized Overachiever

David grew up in Sanford, Florida, a small town where everyone knew everyone. He was always the shortest kid on his team. Picture a kid standing in the outfield, looking like he borrowed his dad's uniform. That was David. But he didn't let his size stop him. He worked harder than anyone else. While other kids were playing video games, David was out in the yard, practicing his swing and fielding grounders. His family supported him, but even they couldn't make him grow taller. Scouts often overlooked him because of his small stature at only 5' 6" tall. Coaches doubted he could compete with bigger, stronger players. But David had a fire inside him. He wanted to prove everyone wrong.

When it was time for high school, David played for the Seminole High School baseball team. Despite his impressive stats and incredible hustle, scouts still didn't pay much attention. It was like he was invisible. But David didn't get discouraged. He kept practicing and playing hard. He knew that one day, someone would see his potential. That moment came when he earned a spot at the

University of Florida. It wasn't handed to him; he had to walk on and prove he belonged. And boy, did he ever. David excelled in college baseball, earning First-Team All-SEC selection in 1995 and 1996. He showed everyone that heart and determination could outshine physical limitations.

After college, David faced another big challenge. He went undrafted. Imagine working so hard, only to see your dreams slip away. But David didn't give up. He signed as a free agent with the Boston Red Sox. He started in the minor leagues, where he had to prove himself all over again. Players bigger and stronger surrounded him, but David's hustle and grit stood out. He worked his way through the ranks, overcoming continuous doubts about his ability to compete at the highest level. His trade to the Anaheim Angels was a turning point. David finally got his shot in the MLB.

David's accomplishments in the MLB are nothing short of amazing. In 2002, he won the World Series MVP with the Anaheim Angels. Imagine being the smallest guy on the team and leading them to a championship. He batted .294 in 16 postseason games, proving that he belonged on the big stage. In 2006, he did it again with the St. Louis Cardinals, earning his second World Series MVP. His key performances helped his team win crucial games. David's hustle and grit made a huge difference. Teammates, coaches, and analysts praised his work ethic and determination. He wasn't just a good player; he was an inspiration.

David Eckstein's story is all about perseverance, hard work, and resilience. He trained relentlessly, always looking for ways to improve. He overcame injuries and setbacks throughout his career, never letting anything keep him down. His acts of sportsmanship and respect for the game earned him admiration from fans and players alike. Off the field, David has been involved in community efforts, inspiring young athletes to chase their dreams, no matter the obstacles.

Reflection Section: What Can You Learn from David Eckstein?

Take a moment to think about David's journey. What challenges have you faced, and how did you overcome them? David's story shows that success isn't just about talent. It's about hard work, perseverance, and staying focused. Write down one or two things you can do to improve your game. Maybe it's practicing your fielding. Also, you can create a list of goals you want to achieve and map out a plan to reach them. Remember, every great player started somewhere, and with dedication, you can achieve your dreams too.

David Eckstein's story is a powerful example of what it means to persevere. From his early days in Sanford to his incredible achievements in the MLB, he showed that with hard work and determination, you can achieve greatness. So, the next time you face a challenge, think about David. Remember that with perseverance, you can overcome anything. Keep pushing, keep playing, and strive to reach your goals.

Ozzie Smith: From Obscurity to the Wizard of Oz

Imagine growing up in Mobile, Alabama, in a big family where you share just about everything, including your love for baseball. That was Ozzie Smith's world. He played in local leagues with his brothers and friends, dreaming of one day making it big. Playing in the dusty fields of Alabama, Ozzie discovered his passion for baseball. He wasn't the tallest or the strongest kid on the team, but he had a spark. He was quick, smart, and had hands like a magician. Still, scouts overlooked him because of his small frame and lack of power. But Ozzie didn't let that stop him.

Ozzie went on to attend Cal Poly San Luis Obispo, where he continued to shine in college baseball. Even though he excelled, many scouts still didn't notice him. They focused on his size rather than his skills. Picture Ozzie, zipping around the field, making impossible plays, but still getting passed over. It was frustrating, but he didn't give up. His determination paid off when he signed with the San Diego Padres. This was his chance to prove everyone wrong and show that being small didn't mean you couldn't be great.

In the minor leagues, Ozzie faced even more challenges. He had to prove his defensive skills and show that he could compete with the best. He struggled at first, but his hard work and dedication started to pay off. Ozzie made an immediate impact with his fielding skills when he debuted with the Padres. Imagine the crowd's reaction as they watched him make jaw-dropping plays. His quick reflexes and smooth moves earned him the nickname "The Wizard." But his journey didn't end there. A trade to the St. Louis Cardinals became the turning point in his career.

With the Cardinals, Ozzie truly became "The Wizard of Oz." His defensive plays were so magical that fans and players couldn't believe their eyes. He won multiple Gold Glove Awards for his excellence in the field. Ozzie's contributions were key to the Cardinals' World Series victory in 1982. He didn't just stop balls; he made unforgettable plays. Picture his iconic backflip before games, energizing the crowd. Or his "Go Crazy Folks" home run in the 1985 NL Championship Series, a moment that still gives fans goosebumps. Ozzie's impact on the game was huge, and his induction into the Baseball Hall of Fame in 2002 sealed his legacy. Ozzie Smith's story is all about perseverance, dedication, and humility. He practiced relentlessly, always striving to improve his fielding. Even when people doubted him, he kept pushing forward. Ozzie overcame early career challenges and proved his critics wrong. His acts of sportsmanship and respect for the game earned him admiration from fans and players alike. Off the field, Ozzie has been deeply involved in community efforts, promoting youth baseball and education. He showed that you don't need to be the biggest or the strongest to make a huge impact.

So, what can you learn from Ozzie Smith? Think about his journey and the challenges he faced. What obstacles have you encountered, and how did you overcome them? Ozzie's story teaches us that success isn't just about talent. It's about hard work, perseverance, and staying focused. Write down one or two things you can do to improve your game. Maybe it's working on your fielding or practicing your throws. Remember, every great player started somewhere, and with dedication, you can achieve your dreams too.

Ozzie Smith's journey from obscurity to becoming "The Wizard of Oz" is a powerful example of what it means to persevere. From his early days in Mobile to his legendary status in the MLB, he showed that with hard work and determination, you can achieve greatness. So, the next time you face a challenge, think about Ozzie. Remember that with perseverance, you can overcome anything. Keep pushing, keep playing, and never give up on your dreams.

Ready to meet more inspiring players who made their mark? Stay tuned for the next chapter, where we explore more stories of incredible athletes who faced challenges and came out stronger. Let's keep the excitement going!

BASEBALL TRIVIA

- Home plate, first base, second base, and third base are in the shape of a diamond. This led to baseball fields being called a diamond.
- The Star-Spangled Banner is sung before every MLB game.
- Most stadiums shoot fireworks after a homerun to fire up the fans.

CHAPTER 16: THE GAME CHANGERS

Ever wondered what it feels like to run so fast that you can't even see your own feet? That's what Rickey Henderson did every time he stole a base. This guy was like a blur on the field, zipping from one base to another before anyone knew what was happening. Imagine playing tag with the fastest kid in school, but you're trying to catch him while he's already halfway to the next base. That's the kind of speed we're talking about here. Rickey turned stealing bases into an art form, and he did it with a swagger that made everyone sit up and take notice.

Rickey Henderson: The King of Steals

Rickey Henderson grew up in Oakland, California, a place where you had to be tough to get by. It wasn't always easy. The neighborhood he lived in had its challenges, but Rickey found a way to rise above them through sports. He played football and baseball in high school, showing off his incredible speed and athletic skills. Imagine being so fast that not even the football players could catch you. That was Rickey. He excelled in both sports, but baseball stole his heart. When the Oakland Athletics drafted him, it was like a dream come true. He saw a chance to use his speed to his advantage on the diamond.

Starting his professional career wasn't a walk in the park. Rickey faced early challenges, including doubts about his abilities. But he didn't let that slow him down. Instead, he used his speed to make a name for himself. He became known for stealing bases, turning what was once a risky move into a game-changing strategy. His determination and grit helped him overcome the early hurdles. He didn't just run fast; he ran smart. He studied pitchers, learned their moves, and figured out the perfect moment to take off.

Rickey's rise to becoming the all-time stolen base leader was nothing short of spectacular. He set the single-season stolen base record with 130 steals in 1982, breaking Lou Brock's previous record. Imagine stealing so many bases in one season that you break a record that everyone thought was unbeatable. Rickey didn't stop there. He went on to break Brock's career stolen base record as well, with his 939th steal. By the time he hung up his cleats, he had a total of 1,406 career stolen bases. That's more bases than some players see in their entire careers!

His base-stealing ability changed the game. Teams started adopting more aggressive base-running strategies because of Rickey's success. He could disrupt pitchers and defenses like no one else. Picture a pitcher sweating bullets, knowing that Rickey is on first and ready to take off. Rickey created scoring opportunities out of thin air, turning singles into doubles and doubles into triples. Teammates, coaches, and analysts praised his game-changing approach. He wasn't just fast; he was smart and strategic.
Rickey's legacy goes beyond just the records. His aggressive base-stealing style influenced generations of players. Kids growing up wanted to be like Rickey, stealing bases and creating chaos on the field. He showed that speed could be just as valuable as power. Rickey's approach to the game made it more exciting and dynamic. Fans loved watching him play because you never knew what he would do next.

Rickey embodied values of innovation, perseverance, and confidence. His work ethic was unmatched. He trained relentlessly, always looking for ways to improve. Early in his career, many doubted him because of his unconventional style. But Rickey proved them wrong time and time again. He played the game with a passion and flair that was contagious. He respected the game and its traditions, always showing sportsmanship on and off the field. Rickey also gave back to the community, inspiring young athletes to chase their dreams.

Rickey Henderson's story is one of speed, strategy, and swagger. He grew up in a tough neighborhood but used sports to rise above his circumstances. Drafted by the Oakland Athletics, he faced early challenges but used his speed to become the all-time stolen base leader. His aggressive base-running changed the game, influencing teams and future players. Rickey's legacy lives on, not just in the record books but in the hearts of fans and young athletes who look up to him.

Mariano Rivera: The Unhittable Closer

Imagine growing up in a small fishing village in Panama. This is where Mariano Rivera's story begins. He was born in Puerto Caimito, a place where baseball wasn't just a game; it was life. Like many kids in his village, Mariano played baseball with whatever he could find. Sometimes, they used milk cartons for gloves and wooden sticks for bats. It was a humble start for someone who would become the greatest closer in baseball history.

Mariano didn't have formal training or fancy equipment. He developed his skills by playing every day and learning from older kids. His talent was raw but undeniable. When the New York Yankees signed him as an amateur free agent, it was the start of something special. But it wasn't smooth sailing. Mariano faced many challenges early in his career. He had to adjust to a new country, learn a new language, and adapt to professional baseball. These obstacles could have stopped him, but Mariano kept pushing forward. He knew he had something special.

Mariano's rise to becoming the greatest closer in MLB history is a story of transformation. Initially, he started as a pitcher, but things weren't clicking. The Yankees saw his potential and moved him to the bullpen as a reliever. This was a game-changer. Mariano found his niche. Then came the moment that would define his career—the discovery of his cut fastball. This pitch was like magic. It moved sharply and baffled hitters. Mariano didn't just throw it; he mastered it. This pitch became his signature move, and it was nearly impossible to hit.

Mariano's career is full of key performances that show why he's the best closer ever. He saved games in the regular season and was even more clutch in the postseason. Imagine standing on the mound with the game on the line, and your team counting on you to seal the win. Mariano did this 652 times, more than anyone else in history. His calm demeanor under pressure was legendary. He made closing games look easy, even when the stakes were sky-high.

Mariano's impact on the game goes beyond just numbers. He redefined what it means to be a closer. Before Mariano, the closer role wasn't as specialized. Teams started to see the value of having a go-to guy to shut down games. Mariano set new standards for the position, and his influence changed how teams managed their bullpens. His ability to stay cool under pressure made him a role model for pitchers everywhere. Teammates, coaches, and opponents praised him for his skill and mental toughness. Mariano's postseason performances are the stuff of legend. He played a key role in the Yankees' multiple World Series victories.

One of the most memorable moments was in the 1999 World Series when he was named the MVP. His dominance in October earned him the nickname "The Sandman," because when he came into the game, it was lights out for the opposing team. Mariano's technique and effectiveness were unmatched. His cut fastball was so good that even when hitters knew it was coming, they still couldn't hit it. Mariano's legacy is built on his ability to perform when it mattered most.

Mariano Rivera embodies the values of perseverance, humility, and excellence. His story is one of continuous improvement and dedication. He didn't become the best overnight. He worked tirelessly, always looking for ways to get better. Even when he was at the top of his game, Mariano stayed humble. He respected the game and its traditions. He played with integrity and always showed sportsmanship. Off the field, Mariano gave back to the community. He started the Mariano Rivera Foundation to help underserved youth. His efforts have made a real difference in the lives of many young people.

Mariano's story is a perfect example of what it means to be great both on and off the field. His journey from a small fishing village in Panama to the bright lights of Yankee Stadium is nothing short of amazing. He faced challenges but never let them stop him. He became the greatest closer in baseball history through hard work, perseverance, and a humble approach. Mariano Rivera's story teaches us that with dedication and the right mindset, we can achieve greatness.

As we wrap up Mariano's incredible story, let's look forward to the next chapter where we dive into the world of champions and learn what it takes to be the best.

WHAT IS A TEAM PLAYER?

A team player is cooperative yet competitive. Always supportive of his/her teammates. A team player must be coachable and willing to learn!

CHAPTER 17: THE CHAMPIONS

Buster Posey: The Heart of the Giants' Dynasty

Ever think about what it's like to be the glue that holds a team together? Imagine being the player everyone looks to for guidance and support. That's Buster Posey. He wasn't just a great player; he was the heart and soul of the San Francisco Giants. But Posey's story starts in a small town in Georgia, where baseball dreams are born.

Buster Posey grew up in Leesburg, Georgia, a place where baseball was more than just a game. In Leesburg, sports were a big deal, and Buster excelled at nearly all of them. Football, soccer, basketball—you name it, he played it. But baseball was his true love. From a young age, he showed a knack for the game that set him apart. He wasn't just good; he was amazing. In high school, he set records left and right. His junior year, he hit a stunning .544 batting average, and as a senior, he smacked 14 home runs. Imagine being the kid everyone talks about because you're that good. That was Buster.

After high school, Buster went to Florida State University. There, he played catcher and first base. His college career was just as impressive as his high school days. He won the Golden Spikes Award and the Brooks Wallace Award in 2008. These are big deals in college baseball. They're given to the best player in the country. It was clear that Buster was destined for greatness. The San Francisco Giants saw this too and drafted him with the fifth overall pick in the 2008 MLB draft. That's like being picked first for kickball, but way cooler.

Once he joined the Giants, Buster didn't waste any time making a name for himself. He zipped through the minor leagues and made his MLB debut on September 11, 2009. But it wasn't all smooth sailing. He faced challenges along the way, like adjusting to the speed and skill of major league pitching. But Buster was determined. He worked hard, studied the game, and soon became a cornerstone for the Giants. His hard work paid off, and it wasn't long before he was leading his team to victory.

Buster's role in the Giants' World Series victories is legendary. In 2010, he helped lead the team to their first championship in over 50 years. He was a rookie, but he played like a seasoned pro. His leadership behind the plate and his clutch hitting were key. He won the National League Rookie of the Year that season. It's like being named MVP of your first Little League season—times a thousand. The 2012 season was another big one for Buster. He not only helped the Giants win another World Series, but he also won the National League MVP. His batting average was a remarkable .336, and he hit 24 home runs. He was on fire, and his team followed his lead.

The 2014 World Series was another highlight. Buster's steady presence and leadership were crucial as the Giants clinched their third championship in five years. He didn't just play; he inspired. His teammates looked up to him, and fans adored him. Whether it was a crucial hit or his spectacular play behind the plate, Buster was always in the thick of things. His impact on the game was clear, and he left a legacy as one of the greatest catchers of all time. But what really sets Buster apart are his values. He's known for his leadership, perseverance, and integrity. He always puts his team first and works tirelessly to improve. He's faced injuries and setbacks, but he never lets them keep him down. He's a true sportsman, always showing respect for the game and his opponents. Off the field, Buster's just as impressive. He's deeply involved in his community and charitable efforts. He and his wife, Kristen, established BP28, a charity for pediatric cancer. They've raised millions of dollars for treatment and research. It's like hitting a home run for a good cause.

Reflection Section: What Can You Learn from Buster Posey?

Think about the challenges you've faced. What did you do to overcome them? Write down one or two things you can do to improve your game. Maybe it's just staying positive when things get tough. Remember, success isn't just about talent. It's about hard work, perseverance, and staying focused. Let Buster Posey's story inspire you to be the best you can be, both on and off the field.

Buster Posey's journey from Leesburg, Georgia, to MLB legend is an inspiring tale of hard work, leadership, and unwavering dedication. He's shown that with determination and a strong set of values, you can achieve greatness. So, the next time you're out on the field, think of Buster. Let his story motivate you to push harder, play smarter, and always strive to be your best.

Madison Bumgarner: The Postseason Dominator

Imagine growing up in a place where fields stretch out as far as the eye can see, and the air smells fresh and earthy. That's Hickory, North Carolina, where Madison Bumgarner was born. From a young age, Madison, or "MadBum" as he's known, showed a love for baseball. But in a rural area, he had to get creative. He practiced pitching by throwing against a barn wall. It wasn't fancy, but it worked. His dad, Kevin, built a mound in their backyard, and Madison spent countless hours there, perfecting his pitch.

In high school, Madison's talent was impossible to miss. He played for South Caldwell High School, where he racked up impressive stats.

He threw fastballs that left batters stunned and hitters shaking their heads. His senior year, he led his team to a state championship. Scouts took notice. They saw a tall, lanky kid with a powerful arm and a fierce competitive spirit. The San Francisco Giants drafted him in the first round of the 2007 MLB draft. Suddenly, his dreams of playing in the big leagues were within reach.

Madison's rise through the minor leagues was swift. He faced challenges, like adjusting to tougher competition and refining his control. But he never backed down. He worked hard, listened to his coaches, and kept improving. By 2009, he made his MLB debut with the Giants. It was a big step, but Madison was ready. He brought the same determination and grit that had defined his journey so far.

Madison's postseason performances are the stuff of legends. In the 2010 postseason, he was just 21 years old. Yet he played like a veteran. He pitched eight shutout innings in Game 4 of the World Series, helping the Giants clinch their first championship since 1954. His calm demeanor and powerful pitches left everyone in awe. The 2012 postseason saw more of the same. Madison continued to dominate on the mound, helping the Giants win another World Series.

But it was the 2014 World Series that cemented Madison's legacy. He delivered one of the most dominant performances in baseball history. In Game 7, he pitched five shutout innings in relief, securing the Giants' victory. His total postseason ERA was a mind-blowing 0.43, a record for pitchers with at least 25 innings. Teammates, coaches, and analysts couldn't stop praising his mental toughness and clutch performances. Madison had become a postseason hero, and his impact on the game was clear.

Madison's career is filled with standout moments. He won the World Series MVP in 2014, a well-deserved honor for his incredible performance. Regular season and postseason games alike showcased his skill and dominance. Whether it was a high-stakes playoff game or a regular season matchup, Madison brought his best every time. His teammates relied on him, and he never let them down. His clutch performances in big games defined his legacy and left a lasting mark on the Giants' success.

What sets Madison apart are his values of perseverance, work ethic, and confidence. He trained relentlessly, always preparing for the next big game. Injuries and setbacks didn't stop him. He faced each challenge head-on, determined to come back stronger.

Madison's sportsmanship and respect for the game were evident in every pitch. He played with integrity, always honoring the traditions of baseball. Off the field, Madison is involved in community efforts, supporting youth baseball programs and inspiring young athletes. His story teaches us that hard work and determination can lead to greatness.

Reflection Section: What Can You Learn from Madison Bumgarner?

Madison Bumgarner's journey from Hickory, North Carolina, to MLB legend is an inspiring tale of hard work, leadership, and unwavering dedication. He's shown that with determination and a strong set of values, you can achieve greatness. So, the next time you're out on the field, think of Madison. Let his story motivate you to push harder, play smarter, and always strive to be your best.

As we wrap up this chapter, think about the champions we've explored. Buster Posey and Madison Bumgarner are stars who led their teams to glory. Their stories connect to the bigger picture of perseverance, leadership, and success. Up next, we'll dive into the unforgettable moments in baseball history. Get ready for some incredible tales that have left a mark on the sport. Stay tuned!

SUCCESS ON THE BASEBALL FIELD

Becoming a successful baseball player takes hard work and dedication. You will not be successful on every play. Occasionally, you will hit a homer! Or a double? Or you will get the "game ball." Other times the ball will pop out of your glove or you'll be "caught looking" for strike 3. This is part of the process of improving. Failure is only a pathway to success!

CHAPTER 18: THE STORIES OF ADVERSITY

Ever felt like you're playing a game with all the odds stacked against you? Imagine having to deal with more than just fastballs and curveballs. Picture growing up in a place where life throws you curveballs every single day. That's exactly what R.A. Dickey faced. He didn't just have to worry about striking out the other team. He had to overcome some serious life challenges just to get on the field. Let's dive into his story and see how he turned those hard knocks into a Cy Young Award.

R.A. Dickey: From Hard Knocks to Cy Young

R.A. Dickey grew up in Nashville, Tennessee. You might think of Nashville as the home of country music, but for Dickey, it was a place filled with challenges. His family life was a mess. His parents divorced when he was young, and his mom struggled with many issues. But the worst part was the extreme troubles he faced as a child. This wasn't the kind of childhood that makes you think of baseball dreams. It was more like a nightmare. Yet, through all the chaos, baseball became his escape. The baseball field was the one place where everything made sense. The rules were clear, the goals were simple: hit the ball, catch the ball, throw the ball. Baseball gave him hope. He clung to it like a lifeline, determined to use the game to rise above his circumstances.

Dickey's determination to pursue his dreams led him to the University of Tennessee, where he played college baseball and majored in English literature. His talent on the mound caught the attention of scouts, and in 1996, the Texas Rangers drafted him. This should have been the start of a smooth ride to the big leagues, but life had other plans. During a routine physical, doctors discovered that Dickey was missing his ulnar collateral ligament (UCL) in his right elbow. For most pitchers, this would be a career-ending diagnosis. But not for Dickey. The Rangers still signed him, but his journey was far from easy. Establishing himself as a traditional pitcher proved difficult, and he struggled to find consistency on the mound.

The turning point came when Dickey decided to transition to a knuckleball pitcher. Now, if you don't know what a knuckleball is, imagine a pitch that seems to have a mind of its own. It wobbles, dances, and makes hitters look silly. But throwing a knuckleball is no easy task. It requires a lot of practice and even more patience. Dickey spent countless hours perfecting the pitch, often facing skepticism from coaches and teammates. The physical and mental toll of his unconventional career path was immense. He had to deal with the frustration of inconsistency and the challenge of mastering a pitch that even seasoned pitchers struggle with.

Despite these challenges, Dickey's hard work began to pay off. He joined the New York Mets in 2010, and by 2012, he had developed and refined his knuckleball to become a dominant pitcher. That year, he had a breakout season, culminating in winning the prestigious Cy Young Award. This award is given to the best pitcher in each league, and Dickey's achievement was historic. He became the first knuckleball pitcher to win the Cy Young Award. His performances included key games where he showcased his effectiveness, such as setting a Mets franchise record with 32 consecutive scoreless innings and throwing two consecutive one-hitters in June 2012. Teammates, coaches, and analysts praised him for his perseverance and skill.

What sets Dickey apart is not just his success on the field but also the way he embodies resilience, determination, and integrity. His unwavering commitment to improvement despite setbacks is a testament to his character. He didn't let personal issues hold him back. Instead, he used his platform to help others. Dickey has been open about his childhood struggles with trauma, and he has used his story to raise awareness and support for victims. He climbed Mount Kilimanjaro to raise funds for victims of human trafficking in India and has been involved in numerous charitable efforts through Honoring the Father Ministries, providing food, medical supplies, and sports equipment to poor communities in Latin America.

Reflection Section: What Can You Learn from R.A. Dickey?

Think about the challenges you face and how you can overcome them. Write down one or two things you can do to improve your game, whether it's practicing a new pitch or working on your swing. Remember, success isn't just about talent. It's about hard work, perseverance, and staying focused. Let R.A. Dickey's story inspire you to push forward, no matter what obstacles come your way.

R.A. Dickey's story is a powerful example of resilience and determination. From his challenging childhood in Nashville to his triumphant rise as a Cy Young Award winner, he showed that with hard work and perseverance, you can achieve greatness. So, whenever you encounter a challenge, let Dickey's journey be your inspiration. Keep in mind that your strength and determination can see you through the toughest times. Continue to strive, stay in the game, and hold fast to your dreams, just as Dickey did.

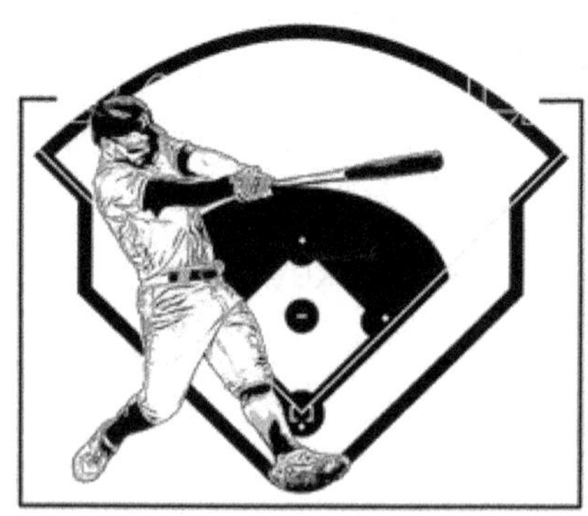

NEGRO LEAGUE TRIVIA

Jackie Robinson, Satchel Paige, and Hank Aaron played in the Negro Leagues.

Satchel Paige and Hank Aaron are from Mobile, Alabama, along with fellow MLB player Ozzie Smith.

Josh Gibson was known as the "Black Babe Ruth".

Many Negro League teams went on "barnstorming" tours.

You can ask your parents to look up "barnstorming" on the internet with you.

CHAPTER 19: THE LEGENDS OF THE NEGRO LEAGUES

Satchel Paige: The Ageless Wonder

Ever wonder what it would be like to throw a baseball so fast that it seems to disappear? Imagine growing up in a place where baseball wasn't just a game but a dream waiting to be chased. That's exactly what happened to Satchel Paige. Born Leroy Paige on July 7, 1906, in Mobile, Alabama, he grew up in a big family where everyone had to pitch in. Satchel worked many odd jobs, from shining shoes to carrying luggage at the train station. But he always found time to play baseball in local sandlots. There, he discovered his amazing talent for pitching. He had a gift for making the ball dance in ways that left batters swinging at air.

As a kid, Satchel often played with his friends using whatever they could find, like sticks for bats and makeshift balls. His natural talent blossomed, and soon he joined semi-pro teams. His performances caught the eye of many, and it wasn't long before he signed with the Chattanooga Black Lookouts, marking the start of his professional career. Life wasn't easy, but Satchel had a fire in him. He knew he was destined for greatness.

Satchel's career in the Negro Leagues took off when he played for the Birmingham Black Barons. He became a sensation with his fastball that seemed to defy physics. He also played for other teams, like the Cleveland Cubs and the Pittsburgh Crawfords. But what really set him apart were his barnstorming tours. Satchel would travel across the country, pitching in exhibition games and wowing crowds with his skill and showmanship. He'd strike out batters and then walk off the mound as if it was no big deal. His confidence was as legendary as his pitches. He even joined the Cleveland Indians, making his MLB debut at age 42. He showed that age was just a number by shutting down batters half his age. Imagine that!

Satchel Paige had many standout moments that solidified his status as a legend. One of his most memorable performances came in 1948 when he pitched a shutout against the Chicago White Sox. His unique pitching style, full of flair and finesse, mesmerized hitters. He could throw a fastball that zipped past batters, then toss a slow, looping curve that made them look silly. Teammates, coaches, and opponents praised his skill and charisma. Satchel didn't just play baseball; he entertained. He became a role model for future generations of pitchers, showing them that it's not just about power but also about style and strategy.

Satchel's values of perseverance, resilience, and showmanship shone through in everything he did. He faced many obstacles, including racial barriers and critics who doubted his abilities. But he never let those challenges stop him. He kept perfecting his craft and stayed competitive well into his 50s. He often said, "Don't look back. Something might be gaining on you." This quote became his mantra, reminding everyone to keep moving forward, no matter what. Satchel also showed great sportsmanship and respect for the game. He was involved in community efforts to promote baseball in underserved areas, inspiring young players to chase their dreams.

Reflection Section: What Can You Learn from Satchel Paige?
Reflect on the hurdles you've encountered in your journey. How have you navigated through them? Satchel Paige faced numerous challenges, including skepticism about his age and abilities, yet he remained undeterred. Jot down a couple of personal obstacles and

your strategies for overcoming them. Bear in mind, achieving success transcends mere talent; it requires dedication, persistence, and a unique spark. Allow Satchel's remarkable story to motivate you to persist relentlessly, regardless of the circumstances.

Satchel Paige's story is a testament to the power of never giving up and always believing in yourself. From his humble beginnings in Mobile, Alabama, to becoming one of the greatest pitchers of all time, Satchel showed us that with hard work and determination, we can achieve greatness. So, the next time you're out on the field, think of Satchel. Remember his incredible journey and let it motivate you to aim high and never give up on your dreams. Keep playing, keep smiling, and most importantly, have fun playing the great game!

Josh Gibson: The Black Babe Ruth

Imagine growing up in a family where baseball is like a second language. That was Josh Gibson's life in Buena Vista, Georgia. Born on December 21, 1911, Josh grew up surrounded by people who loved the game. His family moved to Pittsburgh when he was young, and it was there that his talent started to shine. Playing in local leagues, Josh showed early signs of his incredible power. He could hit the ball so hard, it seemed like it might never come down. At just 16, he joined the Gimbels A.C., and by age 18, he was playing for the Crawford Colored Giants. His talent was clear, but the path wasn't easy. Josh faced many challenges but never let them stop him. He had his eyes set on greatness.

Josh’s determination paid off when he joined the Pittsburgh Crawfords and later the Homestead Grays. These teams were powerhouses in the Negro Leagues, and Josh quickly made a name for himself. His powerful hitting made pitchers nervous. They knew that if they made even a tiny mistake, Josh would send the ball flying out of the park. He faced many obstacles, like racial discrimination and harsh playing conditions. But Josh never gave up. He kept swinging for the fences, determined to prove himself.

Josh Gibson's career in the Negro Leagues was nothing short of legendary. He set home run records that left fans and players in awe. People compared him to Babe Ruth, calling him "The Black Babe Ruth." Imagine being so good that people compare you to one of the greatest players of all time! Josh's home runs weren't just numerous; they were monstrous. Stories of his longest home runs became the stuff of legends. Some say he once hit a ball so far, it still hasn't landed. During exhibition games against Major League players, Josh showed that he could compete with the best. His power at the plate was unmatched, and he left everyone in awe.

Josh’s impact on the game went beyond just his home runs. His hitting ability drew praise from teammates, coaches, and opponents alike. They knew they were witnessing something special. Josh inspired future generations of hitters, showing them that incredible power and skill could come from anyone, regardless of their background. His legacy lived on, even after his untimely death in 1947. In 1972, Josh was inducted into the Baseball Hall of Fame, cementing his place as one of the greatest power hitters of all time.

Josh Gibson's values of perseverance, excellence, and resilience were evident in everything he did. He faced significant racial barriers but never let them define him. Instead, he used those challenges as fuel to push himself even harder. Despite personal and professional challenges, Josh remained focused on his goal of being the best. He displayed acts of sportsmanship and respect for the game, earning the admiration of those who played with and against him. Josh also made efforts to inspire young athletes in the African American community, showing them that anything was possible with hard work and determination.

Josh's story is a powerful example of what it means to pursue excellence, no matter the obstacles. He showed that greatness isn't just about talent; it's about the drive to keep going, even when things get tough. Josh Gibson's legacy continues to inspire and remind us that with perseverance, we can achieve incredible things. His story is one of triumph, not just for himself but for everyone who dares to dream big.

From the streets of Pittsburgh to the Baseball Hall of Fame, Josh Gibson’s journey reminds us that with talent, hard work, and a bit of grit, we can overcome anything. Now, let's move forward to more tales of baseball legends and their unforgettable moments on the field.

RAY
JOSH GIBSON

WHAT ARE YOUR DREAMS?

CHAPTER 20: THE UNFORGETTABLE MOMENTS

The Shot Heard 'Round the World

Imagine a game so intense that it feels like your heart might jump out of your chest. That was the scene during the 1951 National League pennant race. The New York Giants and the Brooklyn Dodgers were fierce rivals, like two heavyweight boxers trading punches. The Giants had trailed the Dodgers by 13 games in August. But guess what? They made a crazy comeback, winning 39 of their last 47 games! This set the stage for a three-game playoff series. The atmosphere was electric. Fans from both sides packed the stadiums, biting their nails and clutching their hats.

The final game of the series was as dramatic as it gets. The score was tight, and the tension was so thick you could cut it with a knife. In the bottom of the ninth inning, the Giants were down 4-2. It seemed like the Dodgers had it in the bag. But then, the Giants started to rally. The crowd was on its feet, and you could hear the buzz of excitement. The Dodgers brought in Ralph Branca to pitch. Up stepped Bobby Thomson. The pitch came, and with one powerful swing, Thomson sent the ball soaring over the left-field fence.

The place went wild. Fans screamed, players jumped, and Russ Hodges, the radio announcer, yelled, "The Giants win the pennant! The Giants win the pennant!" It was a moment of pure joy and disbelief. Thomson's home run didn't just win the game; it became a piece of baseball history. People still talk about it today. It showed how a team can come back from the brink, how teamwork can make anything possible, and how baseball can create moments that last forever.

Reflection Section: Imagine Your Own Comeback Moment
What can you learn from the Giants' comeback and Thomson's home run? How can you apply those lessons to your own life?

Kirk Gibson's Unbelievable Home Run

Picture this: it's the 1988 World Series. The Los Angeles Dodgers, riddled with injuries, are up against the Oakland Athletics. The A's are a powerhouse team, boasting stars like Jose Canseco and Mark McGwire. The Dodgers, on the other hand, are the underdogs. Game 1 is crucial. It sets the tone for the entire series. The Dodgers need something big. But their star player, Kirk Gibson, is injured. His legs are banged up, and nobody expects him to play.

Then, in a move that surprises everyone, manager Tommy Lasorda decides to send Gibson to the plate. The stadium holds its breath. Gibson hobbles to the batter's box, looking like he might fall over any second. The tension is so thick you could slice it with a knife. Facing Dennis Eckersley, one of the best closers in the game, Gibson takes a few uncertain swings. The count goes full. Eckersley throws a backdoor slider. Gibson swings, and the ball rockets into the stands.

The crowd erupts. Vin Scully, the legendary announcer, exclaims, "In a year that has been so improbable, the impossible has happened!" Gibson rounds the bases, pumping his fist. This home run doesn't just win the game. It inspires his team and the fans. It shows everyone that even when you're down, you can still come back. Gibson's determination to play despite his injuries teaches us that perseverance and grit can lead to incredible moments. His home run becomes a lasting memory in baseball history, proving that sometimes, the impossible is possible.

The Miracle Mets of 1969

Imagine being a fan of a team that's, well, not very good. That's what it was like for New York Mets fans before 1969. The Mets were an expansion team, and their early years were rough. They lost a lot, like, a lot. But everything changed in 1969. Manager Gil Hodges took charge, and key players like Tom Seaver and Jerry Koosman stepped up. The Mets started winning games, and fans couldn't believe their eyes. It was like watching a magic trick.

The Mets finished the regular season strong, winning the National League East. They beat the Atlanta Braves in the National League Championship Series, and suddenly, they were in the World Series against the Baltimore Orioles. The anticipation was huge. Fans buzzed with excitement and disbelief. Could the Mets really do this?

In the World Series, Tom Seaver pitched like a hero, while other players delivered clutch hits and made fantastic defensive plays. The final out sealed their victory, and the Mets celebrated like they had just won the lottery. The Miracle Mets showed everyone that belief and teamwork could make anything possible. They started as underdogs but ended as champions.

Lou Gehrig's Farewell Speech

Lou Gehrig was a baseball legend. He was the original "Iron Horse". He played for the New York Yankees and set records left and right. Imagine playing 2,130 games in a row, never missing one! That was Gehrig. But then, something changed. He started to feel weak and tired. Gehrig was diagnosed with Amyotrophic Lateral Sclerosis (ALS), a disease that affects the muscles. He had to retire, and the Yankees held a farewell ceremony for him at Yankee Stadium. The atmosphere was heavy with emotion. Fans, teammates, and the baseball community came together to support him.

As Gehrig took the field for the last time, the stadium fell silent. People knew they were witnessing a historic moment. Gehrig stood there, clearly moved, and then he spoke. "Today, I consider myself the luckiest man on the face of the Earth," he said. His words were filled with gratitude and humility. The crowd erupted in applause, and many had tears in their eyes.

Gehrig's speech left a lasting impact. It showed his courage in facing his illness and his gratitude towards his teammates, fans, and family. His humility touched everyone who heard it. The speech became an inspiration for generations, teaching us the values of courage, gratitude, and humility.

Carlton Fisk's Game-Winning Home Run

Imagine you're in Fenway Park in 1975. It's Game 6 of the World Series. The Boston Red Sox are facing the Cincinnati Reds, known as the "Big Red Machine." The Red Sox have a history of heartbreaks in the World Series. They haven't won since 1918. The Reds are dominant, with a lineup full of stars. The Red Sox need this win to stay in the series.

The game is intense, with back-and-forth scoring. Both teams make key defensive plays and clutch pitches. The tension in the stadium is electric. Every pitch, every swing, you can feel the weight of the moment. Carlton Fisk, the Red Sox catcher, comes to the plate in the 12th inning. He's focused. He's determined. The count is full.

Fisk swings and sends the ball down the left-field line. He waves his arms, urging the ball to stay fair. It hits the foul pole! Fenway Park erupts.

Fisk's home run became one of the most iconic moments in baseball. It changes the game, giving the Red Sox a win and forcing a Game 7. The image of Fisk waving the ball fair is etched in baseball history. It shows the power of perseverance and the drama that makes baseball unforgettable.

The Boston Red Sox Breaking the Curse

Imagine being a Red Sox fan waiting forever for a championship. The "Curse of the Bambino" haunted the team since they traded Babe Ruth to the Yankees in 1919. Heartbreak after heartbreak followed. The Red Sox came close many times but always fell short. By 2004, fans were desperate for a win. That season felt different. The team had stars like David Ortiz and Curt Schilling. They showed grit and determination. The American League Championship Series against the Yankees was epic. Down 3-0, the Red Sox made a historic comeback. Ortiz hit clutch homers, Schilling pitched with a bloody sock, and Pedro Martinez was electric.

The World Series against the St. Louis Cardinals was a breeze. The Red Sox swept the Cardinals in four games. Memorable moments included Manny Ramirez's home runs and Keith Foulke's game-clinching out. The final out led to an explosion of joy. Fans celebrated like never before. The 86-year drought was over. The "Curse" was broken. This win was about more than baseball. It was about perseverance, resilience, and redemption. The players believed in themselves. They battled back from adversity, showing that with determination, anything is possible. This victory gave fans a reason to believe again.

The Chicago Cubs' Historic World Series Win

Imagine waiting over a century to win a championship. That was the life of a Chicago Cubs fan. The "Curse of the Billy Goat" haunted the team since 1945 when a tavern owner and his goat were kicked out of Wrigley Field. The Cubs hadn't won a World Series since 1908. They came close many times but always fell short. The 2016 season felt different. The team had stars like Kris Bryant, Anthony Rizzo, and Jon Lester. They had a dominant regular season, finishing with the best record in baseball. The Cubs plowed through the playoffs, beating the Dodgers in the National League Championship Series.

The World Series against the Cleveland Indians was a nail-biter. It went to a deciding Game 7. The game had everything—lead changes, home runs, and even a rain delay. Dexter Fowler hit a leadoff home run. Rajai Davis tied the game with a homer in the eighth inning. The game went into extra innings. After the rain delay, the Cubs rallied, scoring two runs. They held on to win 8-7. The celebration was epic. Fans cried, hugged, and partied like never before. Ending the 108-year drought showed that with belief and resilience, even the longest curses can be broken.

World Willie Mays' Unbelievable Over-the-Shoulder Catch

Imagine being in a packed stadium in 1954, the air buzzing with excitement. The New York Giants had just clinched the National League pennant after a strong season. They were up against the Cleveland Indians, a team that had set records and dominated the American League. Fans couldn't wait for the World Series to start. The anticipation was through the roof.

The game was tight. In the top of the eighth inning, the score was tied. Then, Vic Wertz of the Indians smacked a powerful hit to deep center field. It looked like a sure double, maybe even a triple. Willie Mays, the Giants' center fielder, sprinted back with incredible speed. He made an over-the-shoulder catch that left everyone in awe. The crowd erupted. This play didn't just save the inning. It shifted the momentum to the Giants.

The Giants went on to win the game and the series. Mays's catch became one of the greatest defensive plays in baseball history. His athleticism was off the charts. The focus and anticipation required to make that catch were unbelievable. This moment showed his excellence and inspired future generations of outfielders. The image of Mays making that catch is etched in baseball lore, embodying the thrill and magic of the game.

Don Larsen's Perfect Game

Imagine the excitement of the 1956 World Series. The New York Yankees and the Brooklyn Dodgers were fierce rivals. The series had been a back-and-forth battle leading up to Game 5. Fans were on the edge of their seats. The air was electric with anticipation. Don Larsen had struggled earlier in the series, but he was determined to bounce back. His teammates and manager believed in him. They knew he had what it took to shine. Larsen focused on every pitch, executing with precision.

As the game unfolded, something magical happened. Larsen was perfect. No hits, no walks, no errors. The stadium was buzzing with disbelief as each out Larsen recorded brought louder cheers. Upon securing the final out, an explosion of joy filled the air. Larsen's teammates hoisted him up in a moment of triumph. This wasn't just any game—it was the first and only perfect game in the history of the World Series. The baseball community was in awe, and Larsen's achievement was immortalized in the annals of the sport. His impeccable focus and precision were on full display, a testament to his skill and determination. Crucial to his success was his synergy with catcher Yogi Berra; their flawless communication and strategy were instrumental. Larsen’s perfect game has become an iconic moment, serving as a beacon of inspiration for pitchers everywhere, showcasing the pinnacle of pitching excellence.

THE ENDURING LEGACY OF BASEBALL S GREATEST PLAYERS

Think about the players we've talked about—Ronald Acuna Jr., Mookie Betts, Mike Trout, Aaron Judge, Shohei Ohtani, and Jose Altuve. These guys aren't just amazing players; they've changed the game. Ronald and Mookie have shown us how to blend power and speed. Mike and Aaron have taught us to never give up, no matter what. Shohei Ohtani and Jose Altuve have expanded the horizons of baseball, proving its universal appeal and global reach. These players have made their mark, inspiring kids everywhere to pick up a bat and dream big.

From these stories, we learn some big lessons. First, perseverance is key. All these players faced challenges but never gave up. Mike Trout didn't let a small-town start stop him. Aaron Judge battled injuries but kept swinging. Second, teamwork matters. None of these players did it alone. They worked with their teammates, lifting each other up. Lastly, integrity and sportsmanship are huge. Whether it's Jose Altuve's smile or Shohei Ohtani's respect for the game, these players show that being a good person matters just as much as being a good player.

These unforgettable moments stick with us. They make us cheer, cry, and feel inspired. Think about Bobby Thomson's miraculous home run. Or Kirk Gibson's legendary swing. These aren't just games. They're pieces of history. The stories of resilience, excellence, and determination shape baseball's culture. They show us that anything is possible if you work hard and believe in yourself. These moments don't just live in the past. They inspire kids, fans, and future stars to chase their dreams and create their own unforgettable memories.

So, as you dream about your own baseball future, remember these stories. Let them inspire you to aim high, work hard, and never give up. Who knows? Maybe one day, your story will be the one inspiring the next generation.

CONCLUSION

Wow, what a journey we've been on together! We've explored the lives of some of baseball's greatest players. From the speed of Rickey Henderson to the power of David Ortiz, we've seen it all. These players faced many challenges. They overcame them with hard work and determination. And let's not forget the fun moments, like clubhouse pranks and unbelievable game-winning plays. Baseball is more than just a game. It teaches us life lessons about perseverance, teamwork, and integrity.

So, what can you take away from these stories? First, remember that everyone faces challenges. Ronald Acuna Jr. had to learn a new language. Mookie Betts had to choose between baseball and bowling. Mike Trout practiced in his backyard with old lights. They all worked hard and never gave up. This shows that you can achieve your dreams too. Stay focused, work hard, and believe in yourself.

Next, think about the importance of teamwork. Baseball is a team sport. No player can win a game alone. Aaron Judge supports his teammates. Clayton Kershaw mentors young pitchers. Buster Posey led his team with his calm presence. Strong teams lift each other up. They work together to achieve their goals. Remember to support your friends and teammates in every aspect of your life. Celebrate their successes and help them through tough times.

Integrity is another key lesson. These players show good sportsmanship. They respect the game and their opponents. Jackie Robinson broke barriers with courage and grace. Roberto Clemente helped others in need. They remind us to play fair and be kind. Always show respect, both on and off the field.

Now, it's your turn to go out and play. Practice your skills and work on your game. Set goals for yourself.

Maybe you want to hit more home runs or improve your pitching. Whatever your goal is, work hard every day to get better. Don't be afraid to ask for help from coaches or teammates. And most importantly, have fun! Baseball is a game to be enjoyed. Laugh with your friends, celebrate your wins, and learn from your losses.

As we wrap up, I want to leave you with a final thought. Baseball has given me so much. It taught me the value of hard work and teamwork. It showed me how to handle setbacks and celebrate victories. I hope this book has inspired you. I hope it has shown you that with perseverance, anything is possible. Whether you dream of playing in the big leagues or just want to be the best you can be, remember the stories of these players. Let them guide and inspire you.

Thank you for joining me on this journey. Keep playing, keep dreaming, and always strive for greatness. Baseball is more than just a game. It's a way of life. And you, my friend, are now a part of it. Go out there and make your own incredible stories. The field is yours.

MOST OF ALL, AS MY OLE FRIEND AND MENTOR DAVID O' WOULD SAY, "IT'S A GREAT DAY FOR THE GREAT GAME!

REFERENCES

- *I Mean No Harm, I Swear | By Ronald Acuña Jr. https://projects.theplayerstribune.com/ronald-acuna-jr-atlanta-braves-mlb-baseball/*
- *Mookie Betts, Los Angeles Dodgers star, describes how his ... https://www.nbcnews.com/news/sports/mookie-betts-los-angeles-dodgers-star-describes-passion-bowling-led-ba-rcna139963*
- *Ronald Acuña Jr. makes MLB.com list of the biggest player ... https://www.si.com/mlb/braves/news/atlanta-braves-ronald-acuna-jr-2023-season-milestones*
- *Mookie and Brianna Betts' 50/50 Foundation makes ... https://www.uclahealth.org/news/article/mookie-and-brianna-betts-5050-foundation-makes-donation-ucla*
- *Mike Trout | Biography, Statistics, & Facts https://www.britannica.com/biography/Mike-Trout*
- *Aaron Judge's Toe "Will Require Constant Maintenance" https://www.si.com/mlb/yankees/news/yankees-captain-aaron-judges-toe-will-require-constant-maintenance-joe9*
- *Mike Trout | Biography, Statistics, & Facts https://www.britannica.com/biography/Mike-Trout*
- *Yankees' Aaron Judge wins MLB's 2023 Roberto Clemente ... https://www.cbssports.com/mlb/news/yankees-aaron-judge-wins-mlbs-2023-roberto-clemente-award-for-community-work/*
- *Shohei Ohtani https://en.wikipedia.org/wiki/Shohei_Ohtani*
- *The Improbable Journey of Houston Astros' Jose Altuve https://bradkyle.substack.com/p/the-improbable-journey-of-houston*
- *Shohei Otani Stats, Age, Position, Height, Weight, Fantasy ... https://www.mlb.com/player/shohei-ohtani-660271*
- *Jose Altuve Delivers Postseason Moment Worthy of His ... https://www.si.com/mlb/2019/10/20/jose-altuve-delivers-postseason-moment-astros-beat-yankees*

- *Juan Soto | Baseball Statistics, Teams ... - Britannica https://www.britannica.com/biography/Juan-Soto#:~:text=As%20a%20boy%20to%20 idolized,creative%20with%20 playing%20 indoor%20 baseball.*
- *Julio Rodríguez's MLB debut | 04/08/2022 https://www.mlb.com/video/julio-rodriguez-s-mlb-debut*
- *Juan Soto Donates All-Star Week Earnings to Dominican ... https://remezcla.com/sports/juan-soto-donates-all-star-week-earnings-to-dominican-athletes/*
- *Seattle Mariners' Julio Rodriguez suffers left wrist fracture https://www.milb.com/news/seattle-mariners-julio-rodriguez-suffers-left-wrist-fracture*
- *Freddie Freeman https://en.wikipedia.org/wiki/Freddie_Freeman*
- *Bryce Harper injury timeline: How Phillies star made ... https://www.sportingnews.com/us/mlb/news/bryce-harper-injury-timeline-phllies-tommy-john-return/hvcy25t5y12nt0k23gf1iy8l*
- *Freddie Freeman wins 2020 National League MVP Award https://www.mlb.com/news/freddie-freeman-wins-2020-national-league-mvp-award*
- *Philadelphia Phillies Superstar Understands How His Play ... https://www.si.com/mlb/phillies/news/philadelphia-phillies-superstar-understands-how-his-play-impacts-this-team*
- *Yordan Alvarez's Family Arrives From Cuba to Watch First ... https://www.si.com/mlb/2022/08/24/family-astros-star-yordan-alvarez-arrives-from-cuba-watch-him-play-mlb-first-time*
- *Gerrit Cole https://en.wikipedia.org/wiki/Gerrit_Cole*
- *Houston Astros: A more vocal Yordan Alvarez emerging as ... https://www.houstonchronicle.com/texas-sports-nation/astros/article/yordan-alvarez-houston-astros-team-leader-18678637.php*

- *Yankees' Gerrit Cole, Wife To Make 'Significant' Donation ... https://www.si.com/mlb/yankees/mlb/yankees/news/yankees-gerrit-cole-significant-donation-coronavirus-relief-nyc*
- *Babe Ruth | Biography, Stats, Nicknames, & Facts https://www.britannica.com/biography/Babe-Ruth*
- *Breaking the Color Line: 1940 to 1946 | Baseball ... https://www.loc.gov/collections/jackie-robinson-baseball/articles-and-essays/baseball-the-color-line-and-jackie-robinson/1940-to-1946/*
- *The Babe's Called Shot https://baseballhall.org/discover-more/stories/baseball-history/called-shot*
- *Jackie Robinson and Civil Rights: From 1947 Until His Death https://sabr.org/journal/article/jackie-robinson-and-civil-rights-from-1947-until-his-death/*
- *Corey Seager - Wikipedia https://en.wikipedia.org/wiki/Corey_Seager#:~:text=Seager%20 began%20his%20professional%20 career,A%20 Midwest%20League%20 for%202013.*
- *Recap of the Historical Rookie Season for Corbin Carroll https://www.si.com/mlb/diamondbacks/analysis/recap-of-the-historical-rookie-season-for-corbin-carroll*
- *Seager, Rangers invest in Senter Park renovation https://www.mlb.com/news/corey-seager-rangers-invest-in-arlington-youth-sports*
- *Corbin Carroll begins recovery from shoulder surgery https://www.mlb.com/news/corbin-carroll-begins-recovery-from-shoulder-surgery*
- *Beyond the hot foot: Enjoy 10 of the greatest clubhouse ... https://www.mlb.com/cut4/beyond-the-hot-foot-enjoy-10-of-the-greatest-clubhouse-pranks-in-mlb-history/c-103639086*
- *50 of the Funniest Moments in Baseball History https://bleacherreport.com/articles/924871-50-of-the-funniest-moments-in-baseball-history*

- *Ranking the 9 Funniest Baseball Players Ever https://bleacherreport.com/articles/1320683-ranking-the-9-funniest-baseball-players-ever*
- *Does pranking improve team culture? https://www.linkedin.com/pulse/does-pranking-improve-team-culture-elaine-jobson-faim*
- *Roberto Clemente - Wikipedia https://en.wikipedia.org/wiki/Roberto_Clemente#:~:text=Born%20in%20 Carolina%2C%20 Puerto%20Rico,Puerto%20Rican%20Professional%20 Baseball%20League.*
- *Cal Ripken breaks Lou Gehrig's record https://baseballhall.org/discover/inside-pitch/cal-ripken-breaks-lou-gehrigs-consecutive-games-record*
- *Roberto Clemente, Humanitarian https://sabr.org/journal/article/roberto-clemente-humanitarian/*
- *Impact https://www.ripkenfoundation.org/about-us/impact*
- *Oh Sadaharu | Biography, Stats, & Facts https://www.britannica.com/biography/Oh-Sadaharu*
- *20 incredible facts about Ichiro's career https://www.mlb.com/news/20-amazing-facts-about-ichiro-suzuki-s-career-c275107436*
- *Japan's Influence on MLB: A Historical Overview https://historicbaseball.com/japans-influence-on-mlb-a-historical-overview/*
- *5 Books About Sports and the Life Lessons They Teach https://nextbigideaclub.com/magazine/5-books-sports-life-lessons-teach/30102/*
- *David Ortiz: From A Dominican Upbringing To 3-Time ... https://www.forbes.com/sites/danschawbel/2017/05/16/david-ortiz-from-a-dominican-upbringing-to-3-time-world-series-champion/*
- *Flashback: Reggie Jackson becomes 'Mr. October' https://www.espn.com/video/clip/_/id/21050644*

- *Three walk-offs in 11 days: How Big Papi built his legend https://baseballhall.org/discover/Three-walk-offs-in-11-days-How-Big-Papi-built-his-legend*
- *Reggie Jackson's three Game 6 home runs lift Yankees to ...* https://baseballhall.org/discover/inside-pitch/reggie-jackson-game-six-hr-lifts-yankees-to-ws-champ
- *Derek Jeter* https://baseballhall.org/hall-of-famers/jeter-derek
- *Dodgers' Max Muncy reveals the truth about Clayton ...* https://clutchpoints.com/dodgers-news-max-muncy-truth-clayton-kershaw-leadership
- *Mission | Derek Jeter's Turn 2 Foundation - MLB.com* https://www.mlb.com/turn-2-foundation/mission#:~:text=The%20Foundation's%20initiatives%20are%20designed,organizations%20that%20support%20its%20mission.
- *Kershaw's Challenge* https://www.kershawschallenge.com/
- *Hank Aaron | Biography, Home Run Record, & Facts* https://www.britannica.com/biography/Hank-Aaron
- *Nolan Ryan amazing stats and facts - MLB.com* https://www.mlb.com/news/nolan-ryan-amazing-stats-and-facts#:~:text=There's%20never%20by%20another%20 pitcher,no%2Dhitters%20and%20324%20 wins.
- *Hank Aaron hits 715th home run, passes Babe Ruth* https://www.mlb.com/news/hank-aaron-passes-babe-ruth
- *A look back at Nolan Ryan's seven career no-hitters* https://mattveasey.com/2023/05/21/a-look-back-at-nolan-ryans-seven-career-no-hitters/
- *David Eckstein - USA Baseball* https://www.usabaseball.com/player/david-eckstein#:~:text=After%20working%20on%20at%20the,Anaheim%20girls%20in%202001%2C%20 batting%20.
- *Wizardry: Ozzie Smith's top 10 career moments* https://www.mlb.com/news/ozzie-smith-top-moments
- *Little big man: Eckstein named World Series MVP* https://www.espn.com/mlb/playoffs2006/news/story?id=2641275

- *Wizardry: Ozzie Smith's top 10 career moments https://www.mlb.com/news/ozzie-smith-top-moments*
- *Rickey Henderson - Baseball Hall of Fame https://baseballhall.org/hall-of-famers/henderson-rickey#:~:text=An%20 accomplished%20running%20 back%20 in,of%2096%20with%20100%20 swipes.*
- *Mariano Rivera https://en.wikipedia.org/wiki/Mariano_Rivera*
- *'gives energy to the whole field': Inside MLB's stolen ... https://www.espn.com/mlb/story/_/id/40797361/it-gives-energy-whole-field-mlb-stolen-bases-resurgence*
- *about mariano rivera https://themarianoriverafoundation.org/mariano/*
- *Buster Posey - Wikipedia https://en.wikipedia.org/wiki/Buster_Posey#:~:text=He%20 attended%20 Florida%20State%20University,debut%20on%20 September%2011%2C%202009.*
- *Madison Bumgarner Career Postseason Stats - StatMuse https://www.statmuse.com/mlb/ask/madison-bumgarner-career-postseason-stats#:~:text=Madison%20 Bumgarner%20had%20a%20 record,the%20 postseason%20in%20his%20 career.*
- *Giants Postseason Results - San Francisco https://www.mlb.com/giants/history/postseason-results*
- *Buster Posey Retires to Focus on Family. Fans ... https://www.kqed.org/arts/13905846/buster-posey-retirement-sf-giants-baseball-mlb*
- *How Mets Pitcher R.A. Dickey Overcame Obstacles On & ... https://skipprichard.com/how-mets-pitcher-r-a-dickey-overcame-obstacles-on-off-the-field/*
- *R. A. Dickey - Wikipedia* https://en.wikipedia.org/wiki/R._A._Dickey#:~:text=a%205.61%20ERA.-,Transition%20to%20the%20 knuckleball,was%20to%20perfect%20the%20 pitch.
- *R.A. Dickey makes history by winning Cy Young in 2012 | Time Machine Tuesday | SNY* https://www.youtube.com/watch?v=7sX5oYCykCU

- *Pro Baller R.A. Dickey Gives Back and Does Good https://inspiyr.com/r-a-dickey-athletes-real-life-hero/*
- *Satchel Paige https://baseballhall.org/hall-of-famers/paige-satchel*
- *Josh Gibson https://baseballhall.org/hall-of-famers/gibson-josh*
- *Integration came at a cost | Negro Leagues | History https://www.mlb.com/history/negro-leagues/features/integration-came-at-a-cost*
- *At Home on the Road https://baseballhall.org/discover-more/history/barnstorming-tours*
- *Bobby Thomson's Shot Heard Round The World https://www.mlb.com/news/bobby-thomson-shot-heard-round-the-world-off-ralph-branca*
- *Inside Kirk Gibson's World Series home run 30 years later https://www.espn.co.uk/mlb/story/_/id/24974235/mlb-kirk-gibson-world-series-home-run-30-years-later*
- *Inside look at the highs and lows of Mets' miraculous 1969 https://nypost.com/2019/06/27/inside-look-at-the-highs-and-lows-of-mets-miraculous-1969/*
- *Fisk, Eastwick recall magical Game 6 in 1975 World Series https://baseballhall.org/discover/museum/whole-new-ballgame/carlton-fisk-and-rawly-eastwick-recall-1975-world-series*
- *https://asmi.org/example-limits-for-number-of-pitches-thrown-in-games/ Lyman S, Fleisig GS, Andrews JR, Osinski ED. Effect of pitch type, pitch count, and pitching mechanics on risk of elbow and shoulder pain in youth baseball pitchers. Am J Sports Med. 2002; 30(4):463-468.*

www.ingramcontent.com/pod-product-compliance
Ingram Content Group UK Ltd.
Pitfield, Milton Keynes, MK11 3LW, UK
UKHW022021190726
13853UKWH00005B/2034

9 798330 559640